THE
MINNESOTA
CHRISTMAS
BOOK

A holly wreath on his head and a sack of toys on his back, Richard Stuefer portrays Father Christmas at Riverplace in Minneapolis, 1984.

THE MINNESOTA CHRISTMAS BOOK

*To Mank and Robin,
May you have a
very merry Christmas
and may the good Spirit
of the north always be
with you.
Charlie Johnston*

Text by Patricia Condon Johnston
Photography by Charles James Johnston

Johnston Publishing Inc.
Afton, Minnesota

Also by Patricia Condon Johnston

Stillwater: Minnesota's Birthplace
Eastman Johnson's Lake Superior Indians
Minnesota's Irish
Pretty Red Wing: Historic River Town

Copyright © 1985
by Patricia Condon Johnston and Charles James Johnston
All rights reserved
First edition
Library of Congress Catalog Card Number 85-090344
ISBN 0-942934-08-3

For our children,

Patty and Jeff
Charles, Jane, and Mary Susan

CONTENTS

*Milk house on the Sundberg farm
at Marine on St. Croix.*

Preface

The first Christmas that Charlie can remember, he and his parents lived upstairs over an old-time sign painter's shop on Selby Avenue in St. Paul. The man painted storefront windows, and Charlie spent a lot of time downstairs, perched on a stool, watching him work out his preliminary patterns. At Christmastime, the man also painted holiday advertising signs for local merchants. Charlie delighted in the blizzard of color that filled the shop; possibly, he'd become a painter himself when he grew up.

In the evenings, back upstairs, Charlie says he liked to lie on his back under the family Christmas tree, looking up at the round glass ornaments. "The closer I put my face to one of them, the bigger my nose looked. Then I'd move back, and my face would get smaller and smaller." But the best thing about Christmas, he decided when he got a little older, was walking downtown to see the Christmas dioramas in the windows at The Golden Rule department store.

"The dioramas were scenes from Dickens's *A Christmas Carol*, and they had small moving parts. I used to stand there an hour or more at a time, utterly entranced. Years later, I went back to the store and asked what had happened to those dioramas, but nobody seemed to know."

In my own house, Christmas was Christmas, but the day after Christmas brought a new flurry of excitement. At least for the female members of the family. My mother liked shopping the after-Christmas sales, and she brought my sisters and me up in the same tradition. When we hit it lucky, we sometimes came home with whole new winter wardrobes. My mother also shopped in earnest for half-price Christmas trimmings.

I don't doubt we had the largest collection of Christmas decorations on the block. Off-season, we stored them in a former billiard room in the basement. (Fortunately, no one in our family ever played pool.) I also remember some pretty spectacular Christmas trees at home. Bachman's brought our tree each year, and they were usually huge pink or white flocked affairs. My mother loved those trees; once she kept one up until Valentine's Day.

Years later, Charlie and I were married at Christmastime. It was the prettiest time of the year for a wedding, I felt. Besides, Charlie was in college and had two weeks vacation. The altar was banked with poinsettias, and the brides-maids wore green velvet dresses and carried white rabbit fur muffs with sprigs of holly. We honeymooned at the Lowell Inn in Stillwater where innkeeper Nelle Palmer always had a showy flocked Christmas tree herself in those years.

But not everybody likes flocked trees, Charlie tells me. He's made it clear that we will never have one. Instead, he brings home a freshly-cut balsam tree each year. It's the *only* kind of Christmas tree as far as he's concerned. We decorate it with ornaments that our family has made and collected through the years. Then I add a few baubles from my mother—glittery whimseys that once hung on earlier flocked trees.

Many people helped us with *The Minnesota Christmas Book*, and we are truly grateful to all of them.

Richard Stuefer, who appears on the cover as Father Christmas, spent the better part of an afternoon posing for Charlie one day last December at River-place. Stuefer makes a specialty of portraying such characters as Old Main Pracna, Voyageur Lucky Pierre, and a riverboat captain for various events on the Minneapolis waterfront. We like his Father Christmas best, of course.

At the Ramsey House, we worked with Site Manager Vera Stanton and Site Technician Rose Amon, both of whom have our admiration for the splendid Christmas program they've devised and supervise. They also provided a wealth of material about the Ramseys and the Ramsey House, and Rose spent off-duty hours helping us get the photographs we wanted.

Lola Perpich was especially gracious when we asked for her help. We're really pleased to be able to follow up Ramsey House traditions with those of our present governor and his family. At the Governor's Residence, we also had help from Vivian Bartsch and Maureen Flahaven.

At the American Swedish Institute, Sherry Younghans provided information concerning the history of the Turnblad house and Swedish Christmas customs. Her colleague, Barbro Roehrdanz, explained Lucia Day traditions. The Lucia Day Breakfast recipes were supplied by Beverly Pratt, curator of the Gammel-garden Museum in Scandia, Minnesota.

Tim Streeter at The Guthrie Theater helped with research material and photographs, and arranged interviews. The *Christmas Carol* photographs on pages 80, 82, and 83 were taken by Joe Giannetti and are used with the Guthrie's permission. Wildlife photographer Jeff Vanuga took the photograph of the ruffed grouse on page 59. His wife (and our daughter), Pat Vanuga, photographed the wolves on page 46.

At Byerly's in Edina, Robert Kinsman made the arrangements that enabled us to include the After-the-Theater Holiday Buffet recipes prepared by Byerly's staff of home economists.

Especially, we applaud our partner in Johnston Publishing, Dale Johnston, who designed this beautiful book. We always look forward to the time when he unveils his design mock-up. This time, we think he outdid himself.
Rohland Wiltfang was production consultant for *The Minnesota Christmas Book*; Evelyn Vida was copy editor.

Lastly, Charlie and I thank our children, Patty, and her husband, Jeff Vanuga, Charles, Jane, and Mary Susan, who make each and every one of our Christmases so very special.

DEAR ALEX

Anna Ramsey knew exactly how she felt about her first Christmas in Minnesota in 1849. She hoped that it would be her last one in this godforsaken place! Pregnant with her second child, Anna was alone in St. Paul with a small son while her husband, Alexander, Minnesota's first territorial governor, remained in Washington. On Christmas Day, a bitterly cold one, she sent him this list of her complaints:

"My dear but very negligent Husband:
". . . Oh, Alex, could thee be here and know how we suffer with cold thee would never want to winter again in St. P[aul]. I know I will not I nearly froze to death in bed as well as out. Today is Christmas and such a one making a shirt for thee and nothing in the house to eat but strong butter and coffee without cream every potato and vegetable is frozen up. . . . My health is not very good I suffer so much with headaches. I do hope thee will hasten home it is such forlorn living alone in such a horrid place as this. I think it intolerable. . . . I made some mince pies last week but [not] having the proper ingredients they are not as good as they might be still they can be eaten. The sleighing on the river is splendid but so cold that one loses all enjoying or at least I do. Sonny enjoys it amazingly if mama will hold him and not let him get cold but unfortunately for him mama is losing her lap. The thermometer stands at 22 degrees below zero and if it gets much colder I shall have to close the house as the four windows and five doors besides innumerable cracks give more air than we really require. . . . I tell thee now thee shall never leave me again so long. I will not stay."

The next Christmas, Alexander Ramsey's first in Minnesota, was a better one for the family. The governor had purchased the lot on the corner of Walnut and Exchange streets (where the Ramsey House now stands) and built what visiting author Fredrika Bremer called "a handsome spacious house." Guests at the Ramseys' Christmas table in 1850 dined on a saddle of venison, and Alexander wrote in his diary that he received gifts of "a fine long sleeved pair of fur gloves and a pretty segar case." A neighbor presented Anna with a "very handsome painting in a gilt frame [of a] lady shading her face with a fan."

In the years that followed, Ramsey proved himself not only a popular politician but a shrewd businessman (who knew a choice piece of real estate when he saw one). In 1868, after deciding that his improved status and increased fortune required a larger and more prestigious homestead, he moved his first-built house across the street to make room for the present Ramsey House.

While her husband saw to it that their new fifteen-room limestone mansion went up according to his grandiose designs (Ramsey specified no fewer than seven white marble fireplaces and insisted on such innovations as central heating and indoor plumbing), Anna shopped for furnishings in New York. Her purchases filled two train cars and set Ramsey back fifteen thousand dollars. This included the rosewood Steinway concert grand piano still played at the Ramsey House each year during the holidays.

Like the Ramsey House itself, Christmas traditions in the residence remain unchanged from the 1870s. During the holidays, formal parlor dances are held in this front parlor.

When the last of the black walnut woodwork had been stained and varnished, the richly-patterned Oriental carpets laid, and the Bohemian crystal chandeliers hung in place, Anna Ramsey threw open the doors of her elegant residence for a public party on December 20, 1872. The affair was a benefit "musical sociable" that netted seventy-five dollars for the House of Hope Presbyterian Church. Anna's holiday bash also marked the beginning of a new era. The massive French Renaissance house might be Ramsey's personal monument to his enormous success, but it was likewise the cornerstone for the fashionable Irvine Park neighborhood that grew up around it.

While Irvine Park has had its ups and downs during the past hundred years, the Ramsey House remains virtually unchanged. Alexander Ramsey and his family were its sole occupants. In 1875 the Ramseys' daughter, Marion, was married to Charles Furness from Philadelphia in the front parlor. (Marion was the only one of the Ramseys' three children to survive childhood.) The bride's trousseau was from Paris, and the Belgian lace fan she carried, with its ivory sticks on pearl mounts, is preserved in the room.

The young couple moved to Philadelphia, but early in the marriage Furness developed medical problems that required him to be hospitalized for the rest of his life. As a result, Marion was often at her parents' home with her three children, Anita, Ramsey, and Laura. After Anna died in 1884, Marion stayed on permanently. For the next nineteen years, until Governor Ramsey's death in 1903, she was her father's hostess.

There were frequent parties for the children during these years, especially at Christmastime when the decorated tree in the parlor nearly reached the fourteen-foot ceiling. For Christmas, 1887, Marion gave her daughter Laura the dollhouse (displayed in the third-floor playroom) that is a replica of the governor's mansion. Many of its furnishings are the original ones. Other pieces have been added from the toy collection of the Minnesota Historical Society which now administers the Ramsey House.

Both Ramsey granddaughters, Anita and Laura Furness, had coming out parties at the house, but neither of them ever married. After their mother died in 1935, both sisters lived out their lives in the family home. Most of the furnishings at the Ramsey House, down to the monogrammed Haviland china and ornate silver hollowware, belonged to the Ramsey family. Come Christmastime, bedecked from top to bottom with traditional trimmings, the Ramsey House is a stunning showcase for the holiday at its nineteenth-century best.

The twelve-foot tree in the parlor is decorated with candles in clip-on holders and Ramsey family ornaments (one of which appears to be a gilded almond and opens to reveal one-hundred-year-old candies). In Governor Ramsey's former library, the Furness children have hung up their stockings by the fireplace. For added good measure, there's even a boxwood kissing ball suspended from the chandelier in the front hall. Made fresh yearly, it is a perennial favorite with guests who often kiss each other under it.

The Christmas stockings are for Governor Ramsey's three grandchildren, Anita, Ramsey, and Laura Furness. The portrait to the right of the fireplace depicts Anna Ramsey's paternal grandmother, Mary Hutchinson Jenks. Governor Ramsey is pictured in the photograph.

Dressmaker Jim Morehouse makes the elaborate 1870s dresses worn by tour guides at the Ramsey House. Formerly a guide himself at the house, Morehouse has set up shop as J. M. Costumer in the basement of his home in Inver Grove Heights. The machine he uses is a 1921 Singer treadle model that was his great-grandmother's ("I wouldn't give it up for anything," he says). Morehouse's dresses for the Ramsey House this season included a stylish moire and velvet visiting outfit in warm browns, and a slightly frillier gray silk and taffeta carriage outfit.

Morehouse majored in theater in college and has been sewing professionally for six years. He learned to put Victorian clothing together by examining the clothes still intact in the Ramsey House closets, he says. (Marion's wedding dress, for instance, which she had made over for dressy occasions, can be seen in her former room.) "All my techniques come from what I saw inside those outfits."

During the holidays at the Ramsey House, Morehouse is often backstage, so to speak, making sure that the guides are all "proper Victorian ladies." He shows them how to sit in a bustle dress and how to make turns with trains. "You can't simply about-face in a train and walk in the opposite direction," he tells them. "You'll trip on the train." The guides needle him about the bustles he constructs in the dresses. "They tell me they have enough back there already!"

Special Christmastime programming at the residence includes a series of formal parlor dances during evening tours. The Ramseys themselves once hosted these kinds of gatherings. The dances were known colloquially as "Germans;" actually, they were quadrilles and depended upon patterns and partners. Somewhat less formal than minuets, they were very popular in the 1870s and 1880s. A local amateur dance group recreates these dances at the Ramsey House, down to the costuming.

In the Ramsey House kitchen, holiday visitors sample freshly-baked ethnic delicacies. Guest cooks prepare the recipes on weekends, and these same recipes are repeated by Ramsey House guides during the following week. Ethnic cookery is featured because St. Paul welcomed many thousands of immigrants during the time that the Ramseys lived in the community. The Ramseys mingled and did business with people of numerous nationalities.

Guided tours of the Ramsey House (which is open to the public ten months of the year, closing in January and February) begin with an orientation show in the reconstructed carriage house on the grounds. The original carriage house, built in 1883, was torn down in 1920. Fortunately, the plans survived and the Historical Society had it duplicated in 1970. Not incidentally, this structure also houses a Victorian gift shop.

Be it ever so splendid, there's no place quite like the Ramsey House at Christmastime. The very memory of Anna Ramsey's first cold Christmas in Minnesota is forgotten. Indeed, the holiday has never looked more at home.

Dressmaker Jim Morehouse sews
an 1870s carriage outfit for a
Ramsey House tour guide. Boned
and bustled, the finished ensemble
will be worn with a derby style hat
(also by Morehouse) with ostrich
feathers and long gray ribbons.

The Ramseys' holiday table,
complete with plum pudding. The
portraits are of Anna Ramsey's
parents, Thomas and Mary Jenks.

A CHRISTMAS PLUM PUDDING

8 oz. mixed candied fruit
4 oz. candied citron
4 oz. candied pineapple
½ cup walnuts
¼ lb. suet
1 cup currants
1½ cups raisins
1 tbsp. cinnamon
1½ tsp. ground ginger
¼ tsp. nutmeg
½ tsp. allspice
¼ tsp. salt
1 cup sugar
½ cup strawberry preserves
1½ cups dry bread crumbs
4 eggs
2 tbsp. milk
½ cup brandy
½ cup sherry
½ cup brandy for flaming (if desired)

Finely chop candied fruit, citron, pineapple, walnuts, and suet. In large bowl, combine fruit, citron, pineapple, walnuts, suet, currants, raisins, spices, salt, sugar, preserves, and bread crumbs. In a second bowl, beat eggs until very thick. Beat in milk, brandy, and sherry and blend well. Add egg mixture to fruit mixture and mix well.

Turn batter into well-greased 1½ quart pudding or pyrex mold. Wrap the mold with several layers of cheesecloth, tying cheesecloth around top with string. Place the mold on a trivet in a deep kettle and pour in boiling water to come half way up side of mold. Cover kettle and steam four hours with water gently boiling.

Serve hot with hard sauce or wrap in foil and store in cool place (up to thirty days).

Hard Sauce

⅔ cup butter, softened
2 tsp. vanilla extract
2 cups unsifted confectioners' sugar

Cream butter until light. Add vanilla and sugar. Beat until fluffy. (May be made one or two days before serving.)

Also: If you would like to set pudding aflame before serving it, warm brandy in a small saucepan over low heat, ignite it with a match, and pour it flaming over the pudding.

Louis Sonnen at the organ at
Assumption Catholic Church.

GLORIA IN EXCELSIS DEO

At the Organ: Louis Sonnen

In downtown St. Paul, Louis Sonnen has been the organist at the Assumption Catholic Church for fifty-eight years. His wife, Rosabelle, and the couple's five children and their families sing in the choir which he conducts as well. The Midnight Mass they perform on Christmas Eve will likely be a Mass that Sonnen also composed.

Louis Sonnen grew up in Assumption parish and graduated from Assumption School in 1925. He has always been musically inclined, but his father, a druggist, didn't want him to have piano lessons. Instead, his sister ("who couldn't care less about music," he says) took the lessons. "I used to listen to her practicing on the piano downstairs and play the same thing by ear on an old organ my mother had upstairs."

Louis was fourteen years old and still without a lesson the first time he played the organ for Midnight Mass at the Assumption. He was head altar boy ("because I was the tallest") and was supposed to lead the procession that evening. But with the ceremony ready to begin, the organist still hadn't showed up. He was scared to death, Sonnen recalls, but he volunteered to go up into the choir loft and play the organ. After that, Sister Johanna, a Notre Dame nun who taught piano at the Assumption School, gave him lessons. Later, he also studied at MacPhail School of Music in Minneapolis.

In the early 1960s, when the first Masses were being said in English, Sonnen began writing music for them. There was a dearth of published music for English Masses at the time, and some of what was available was very poor, he says. His most recent Mass was written as a tribute to Sister Johanna (who remained a lifelong friend and corresponded with Sonnen until her death in 1983); it commemorates the feast of her patron saint, St. John the Baptist.

Sonnen's paternal grandparents were German immigrants who came to St. Paul from New Ulm following the Indian attack on the town in 1862. He married Rosabelle (whose parents emigrated from Luxembourg) at the Assumption in June, 1940. "I met the darling in the choir," he says. "Both she and her sister sang in the choir, and I had to take them both out because I didn't know which one I wanted." It didn't take him long to make up his mind, however; nine months later he wed Rosabelle.

Outside Assumption parish, Louis Sonnen is best known for the pet shop he still operates with his son, David, on St. Peter Street in St. Paul. (Sonnen's Pet Shop celebrated its fiftieth anniversary in 1984.) Oddly enough, the shop seems to have picked Sonnen, not the other way around.

Hired by the widow of the former proprietor, Sonnen took a job there during the Depression in 1931 at six dollars a week, only to quit after the first day. "I couldn't stand the animal smell," he says. The woman raised his pay to seven dollars and he tried again, but "I just couldn't take it at all." By Saturday, she was offering him fifteen dollars a week.

"Married people weren't getting much more than that, and my parents would have been furious if I hadn't stayed," he says. Shortly after that, the woman's health failed and she had to sell the shop. Sonnen bought it, but then and there he stopped handling dogs and cats. Instead, he sells birds and fish and pet supplies.

During the early years of their marriage, Louis and Rosabelle came downtown by streetcar on Christmas Eve for Midnight Mass at the Assumption. After they got home at two or so in the morning, they would put up the Christmas tree. "Santa Claus always brought the tree in the middle of the night," he says. In the morning, each of the children came down to find his or her own chair piled with gifts, remembers daughter Rosemary. "Daddy didn't just set out the presents. They were all *displayed*.

"You're looking at 'Mr. Christmas,' " says Rosemary. In addition to seeing to it that the holiday receives the proper attention at home, Sonnen trims the downtown pet shop to a fare-thee-well each year. Two days before Christmas, the Sonnen family, under Sonnen's direction, also decorates the Assumption Church. This includes cleaning the altar, arranging poinsettias, hanging wreaths, and setting up the stable with its nearly life-size figures. Last year, Sonnen shopped five Twin Cities Christmas tree lots to find the right trees for the main altar.

The interior grandeur of the Assumption, incidentally, remains undiminished in the wake of Vatican II; it is a glorious church, proud of its time-honored statuary, with the look and feel of the last century. Originally a German parish, the present church was built beginning in 1870 and is patterned after von Gaertner's famous Ludwigskirche (Ludwig's Church) in Munich. The organ that Louis Sonnen plays, built by the Odenbrett and Abler Company of Milwaukee, was installed in 1883 and has twenty-nine speaking registers consisting of 1,658 pipes. The best that could be had, it cost the parish $4,300.

In recent years, Midnight Mass on Christmas Eve at the Assumption has been celebrated at eight o'clock in the evening. This is mainly to accommodate the many older people living in the parish. Before the service, Sonnen conducts the choir in a half-hour program of Christmas music. Later in the evening, following Communion, it is traditional at the Assumption to dim the lights, except for a spotlight on the stable, while the choir sings "Silent Night" in German. (This brings tears to not a few eyes.) Then the lights are turned up and the congregation joins the choir in the English version of the hymn.

It's been many years since Louis Sonnen has lived within the boundaries of Assumption parish. The Sonnens and all five of their children and their families, in fact, live in Nativity parish in St. Paul. Their youngest daughter, Susan, is still at home. The other four children (Louise, David, Rosemary, and Eugene) all have homes within a couple of blocks of their parents. "We always liked going downtown to the Assumption when we were kids," says Rosemary. "We called it 'Daddy's organ church.' "

Rosemary, whose middle name is Carol, was born just around the corner from Assumption Church at St. Joseph's Hospital on Christmas Eve in 1945. It was one of the busiest days of his life, says her father. The pet shop was doing its best business of the year. And he was back and forth between the shop and the hospital all day. But that evening, who, pray tell, was at the organ for Midnight Mass?

If you guessed Louis Sonnen, you're getting the picture.

St. Peter's Catholic Church in Mendota, built in 1853 from native limestone by French missionary Augustine Ravoux and his parishioners, is the oldest church in continuous use in Minnesota.

Christmas: The Upside-Down Holiday

"Christmas is the upside-down holiday," the Reverend Mr. Calvin Didier told his congregation last year. Didier is pastor of House of Hope Presbyterian Church in St. Paul and one of the most popular churchmen in Minnesota. One thing his parishioners have come to expect in his homilies is the unexpected.

"When Alice walked through the mirror into Wonderland, she found a bottle that said, 'Drink me,' " he began this particular Sunday in Advent. "As soon as she had drunk the liquid, she grew smaller and smaller until she could go through the keyhole into that world where reality became fantasy and everything was reversed.

"Christmas is our keyhole to enter a different world," he continued. "Once you step into Bethlehem's stable, all values are reversed. You find yourself in a spiritual dimension where the big things are little, the little things big, the strong weak, and the weak turn out to be the most powerful influence in the world."

Rather than treat Christmas as a quaint expression of an ancient celebration in the church's life, Didier says that he wants to make it something that's relevant in our lives today. "It's wonderful, the business of carrying on a tradition and so on, but the whole thrust of my job is to try to contemporize a thing. What does it mean today?"

Carrying his theme a step further, Didier explains that the Messiah was expected to be a powerful political leader. "And yet, in this upside-down world of the manger, a baby was proclaimed Savior of the World." He also suggests that people tend to see God as the villain should disaster befall them. But at the end of the story, who is it who's hanging on the cross?

"But let's not rehearse the obvious details. A deeper consideration of Christmas demonstrates that whatever God touches—like Alice's magic potion—that place, that person is turned upside-down. Christmas changes all human values. It changes all human goals and directions. It will change our lives if we let it."

Summarizing Didier's meditations is hardly to do them justice. He is a scholarly man and quick-witted; his presentations are low-key but lively. "I decided long ago that I would do everything I could to break out of the normal mold of expectation," says Didier. "I did not want to indulge in the sensational, but at the very least I wanted to keep people awake."

Mr. Didier was recruited for the House of Hope by a delegation led by Frederick Weyerhaeuser in 1970. Prior to that, he was "Executive Pastor" (a title that seems to embarrass him) at Redfield Presbyterian in Detroit. It was a well-endowed parish, supported by auto industry VIPs. Earlier, he had ministries in Indiana and Ohio.

Pastor Calvin Didier in his office at the House of Hope Presbyterian Church on St. Paul's Summit Avenue.

Growing up in Michigan, Didier remembers handing bowls of soup through the windows of the local Buick plant to workers involved in some of the first sit-down strikes. Both his father and maternal grandfather were Presbyterian ministers. His two brothers likewise entered the ministry. Didier trained at McCormick Theological Seminary in Chicago and also has an MA in English Literature, earned at the University of Michigan.

Much of the history of the House of Hope Church and its traditions center around Christmas. The parish was founded on Christmas Eve, 1855, by Presbyterian missionary Edward Duffield Neill from Pennsylvania. Neill and his wife, Nancy, both in their twenties, had arrived in St. Paul in 1849, the same year as the Alexander Ramseys. Governor Ramsey was a trustee in the church and an elder. By 1858 the congregation had built a small cabin-like frame church at Walnut and Oak streets.

Judging by what he accomplished, the Reverend Dr. Neill, a graduate of Amherst, was an extraordinarily capable man. In addition to founding the House of Hope, he had earlier established First Presbyterian Church in St. Paul in 1849. Dr. Neill was Minnesota's first superintendent of public schools and the first chancellor at the University of Minnesota. He also founded Macalester College. The Neill family home was the first one on what later became Summit Avenue; it stood on the present site of the James J. Hill mansion.

On Christmas Day, 1869, fourteen years after its inception, the House of Hope held its first services in a new and far more elegant church (it even had a steeple) at Fifth and Exchange streets. The building site was supplied by Alexander Ramsey. Shortly after the turn of the century, First Presbyterian and House of Hope churches merged and built the present Gothic-style House of Hope Church at Summit Avenue and Avon Street in 1914.

In 1978 Pastor Didier and the House of Hope made *The New York Times* when a minor miracle of sorts occurred, possibly with Didier's help, on Christmas Eve and right in his own sanctuary. All was in readiness for the eleven o'clock evening service when the so-called "kissing bell" from Macalester College was discovered in the sanctuary. This was no small matter; the kissing bell weighs six hundred pounds.

Didier immediately took advantage of the situation by scrapping his prepared sermon to talk about the bell. It seems that the bell had originally belonged to the House of Hope. It had been given to Dr. Neill by a friend in Philadelphia and hung in the second House of Hope Church at Fifth and Exchange streets. Later, when the present church was erected, it included a tower for a carillon and the bell was superfluous.

So the bell was sent over to Macalester where it was stored in the basement of the school's Carnegie Science Hall. Some ten years later, a group of Macalester students put up a cupola to house it, and the bell has since become a college landmark. (Once the bell was installed at Macalester, the tradition of kissing under it also took hold.) So how did the kissing bell make its way into Mr. Didier's sanctuary?

"Some people brought it here and delivered it," is as much as he says he knows. But seeing as it was on the premises that night, the pastor suggested that if Macalester would like to have it returned, perhaps they could send a delegation to the church to claim it. At such time as the Macalester group outnumbered the people in his church, they could have the bell back, he offered.

"It was a way of poking Macalester in the ribs," says Didier. "I was saying, 'Hey, you guys claim to be Presbyterians and you claim to support the church and want its financial resources. How about some relationship with its spiritual origins?' The connection between the church and the college had pretty much disappeared."

Carved in stone, this angel decorates the exterior facade of St. Luke's Catholic Church, built on the corner of Summit Avenue and Lexington Parkway in St. Paul in 1926.

Back at Macalester, however, officials had discovered the bell missing and reported the caper to the police. Once they learned of its whereabouts, there was talk of a lawsuit. "There wasn't anybody over there who thought it was funny," says Didier. *The New York Times* reporters thought it was terribly funny, and Macalester's own lawyer thought it was funny, but Macalester's leadership at that time didn't." The day after New Year's, the college sent its custodians over to House of Hope with a truck to collect the bell.

Traditionally, parishioners at House of Hope celebrate the birth of the Christ Child each year with a Christmas pageant at the five o'clock Christmas Eve Candlelight Service. This custom dates to 1923 when the program was first arranged by member Grace B. Whitridge (who was also on the faculty at Macalester). Some people in the parish have taken part in the program nearly every year since.

Accompanied by the House of Hope Choir, parishioners present the Christmas story as told in the Scriptures, illustrated with tableaux based on familiar Christmas paintings. Church elders read the prophesies, and other members portray scenes from masterworks by Fra Angelico, Ghirlandajo, Rembrandt, and Giorgione. All of this takes place in the sanctuary. The response to this program is such that Didier says he often thinks of holding two services to accommodate the people.

One Sunday morning in Advent, the House of Hope also presents a Christmas Cantata or similar musical program in place of the usual Sunday service. Professional musicians from the Minnesota Orchestra and the St. Paul Chamber Orchestra accompany the House of Hope Choir. "This is something new," says Didier. "Years ago churches hesitated to include a program like this in the service. They always put it on as something extra." Didier prefers to take advantage of the audience he already has in church. He also likes good music. Last year's program was *Fantasia on Christmas Carols* by Ralph Vaughan Williams.

Mr. Didier's meditation that day was about angels. He quoted G. K. Chesterton: "Do you know why angels can fly? Because they take themselves so lightly." This led to a discussion of some practical applications of good will on earth.

He also took a few minutes to introduce the music. Vaughan Williams was related to the Wedgwood china people, he said, but also to Charles Darwin. As a boy, the composer had questioned his mother about his relative's unorthodox views on creation. This needn't concern him, his mother told him. "The Bible says that God made the world in six days. Great Uncle Charles thinks it took longer, but we need not worry about that.

"It is equally wonderful either way."

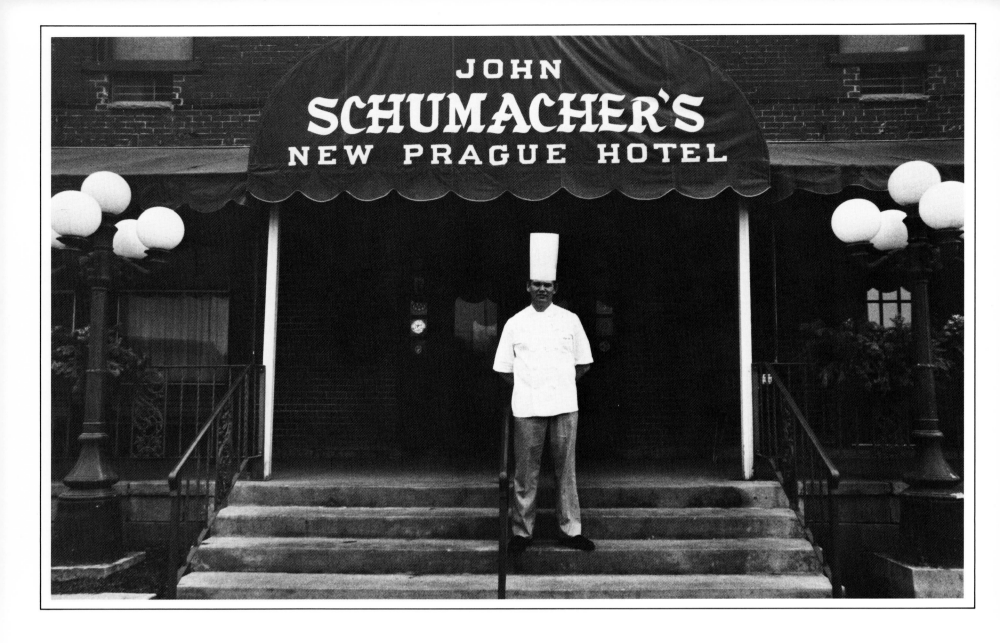

John Schumacher Cooks Christmas Eve Supper

John Schumacher's New Prague Hotel is the former Broz Hotel, designed by Cass Gilbert and built in New Prague in 1898. Since John Schumacher bought the hotel in 1974, he has also established an enviable culinary reputation for this historic inn. The hotel itself has been refurbished and furnished with antique and hand-painted furniture to resemble a Bavarian or Austrian hostelry. But it's John Schumacher's cooking that has made the real difference.

In a recent article touting the inn, *Gourmet* magazine called Schumacher "the hotel's finest asset, a dynamic, opinionated and talented Minnesota farm boy [he grew up in Wheaton], who never imagined he would spent his days—and nights—making schnitzel and strudel." John graduated from the Culinary Institute in Hyde Park, New York, and specializes in Czech-German cooking. (New Prague is a Czechoslovakian community, "so it just seemed the right thing to do," says John.)

Note: John suggests that when you follow his recipes, you adjust the seasoning to your personal taste. Also, when I asked him why the herring salad was listed near the end of the menu, he said that in Europe the salad course customarily follows the entree. It could also be used as an appetizer, he said.

One of Minnesota's best-known chefs, John Schumacher, in front of the historic hotel he has restored in New Prague.

MENU

Goulash Soup
Chicken With Mushrooms
Potato Dumplings
Sauteed Cabbage
Creamed Green Peas
Smoked Herring Salad
Fruit Cream Dessert
Wine Suggestion:
Any dry white wine or
Pilsner Urquell Czechoslovakian Beer

Goulash Soup

2 onions, chopped
2 tbsp. butter
¼ tsp. paprika
1 lb. diced beef
  (chuck or shank)
¼ cup butter
¼ cup flour
6 cups boiling water
1½ cups diced vegetables
  (carrots, parsnips, celery)
  salt to taste
1 lb. diced potatoes
¼ tsp. caraway seeds
  dash pepper

Fry onion in the 2 tbsp. butter. Add paprika and meat. Cook slowly until brown (about 30 min.). Melt the ¼ cup butter, blend in flour, and fry until golden, stirring constantly. Add to meat with water, vegetables, and salt. Simmer for 20 minutes. Add potatoes, caraway seeds, and pepper, and simmer until potatoes are tender (20-30 min.). Serves 4 to 6.

Chicken With Mushrooms

2 small chickens
½ cup butter
1 large onion, chopped
1 cup mushrooms, sliced
  salt to taste
1½ cups water
1 cup sour cream
1 tbsp. flour

Cut chicken into small pieces and brown in butter. Add onion; wilt; add mushrooms, salt, and water. Cover and simmer until tender (about 45 min.). Remove chicken from pan. Mix sour cream and flour together, blend into pan juices, and bring gravy to a boil. Serve with chicken.

Potato Dumplings

2 lbs. potatoes, peeled
salt to taste
1 egg
3 cups flour

Grate raw potatoes; drain. Add salt, egg, and flour. Mix well. Drop by spoonfuls into boiling salted water; cook 6 to 8 minutes. Make sure dumplings do not stick to the bottom of the pan. Remove with a skimmer.

Sauteed Cabbage

1½ lbs. cabbage, shredded
1 cup water
1 medium onion, chopped
½ cup lard
½ tsp. caraway seeds
salt to taste
1-2 tsp. sugar
juice of 1 lemon
(or vinegar to taste)
2 tsp. flour

Simmer cabbage in water for about 5 minutes. Add onion browned in lard (drain lard), caraway seeds, and salt, and saute 10 to 15 minutes. Add sugar, lemon juice or vinegar, and flour; simmer for 5 minutes. Serves 4 to 6.

Creamed Green Peas

1 lb. fresh green peas
(2 cups shelled)
½ cup salted boiling water
¼ cup butter
½ tsp. sugar
salt to taste
pepper to taste
dash nutmeg
1 cup cream
2 tbsp. flour
1 tbsp. minced parsley

Simmer peas in water for 5 minutes. Drain. Saute with butter and sugar until tender (5-15 min.). Stir in seasonings and cream mixed with flour; simmer for 3 minutes. Before serving, add parsley.

Smoked Herring Salad

½ lb. smoked herring,
  boned and diced
½ lb. potatoes, cooked and diced
1 small onion, chopped
1 cup mayonnaise
  lemon juice to taste

Blend all ingredients. Mound in lettuce cups.

Fruit Cream Dessert

1 cup milk
2 egg yolks
¼ cup sugar
1 tbsp. cornstarch
2 tbsp. cognac
2 cups whipped cream
⅔ cup chopped toasted nuts
1 orange, sliced
½ cup candied cherries
½ cup grapes

Mix together milk, egg yolks, sugar, and cornstarch. Bring to a full boil, stirring constantly. Cool. Add cognac and half the whipped cream. Fold in nuts and fruit. Pour into a mold and chill until firm. Decorate with the remaining whipped cream.

TOYS, DOLLS, AND MORE DOLLS

Mary Ann Scroggins's Afton Toy Shop

Charles Dickens suggested that "it is good to be children sometimes, and never better than at Christmas." If that is the case, there is probably no easier jumping-off place than Mary Ann Scroggins's Afton Toy Shop.

Housed in a single-story 1850s frame house on Afton's main street, this is a toy shop with a difference. For starters, none of its toys are advertised on television. Instead, Mary Ann shops the world to find the myriad well-designed (and always beguiling) toys she stocks from thirty-nine countries. Many of these hand-picked toys are produced by small cottage industries. All of them have been selected for aesthetic as well as practical reasons.

"Of course, most toys are art to me," Mary Ann explains. They're also her passion: "If I find something in any area of toys that has a special appeal for me, I have to have it." Of late, she admits to being on a top "kick." "Anytime I find a new kind of top or a new version of an old kind of top, I find it very exciting." For umpteen years she has also been adding to her prized collection of toy Santa Clauses.

Mary Ann opened the Afton Toy Shop in 1976 to help preserve what she considered an endangered species. "I just felt that because of the pressures of the market, good toys were dying out." A good toy doesn't need a lot of hype, she contends. It exists on its own merits. Mary Ann also feels strongly that toys should be built to last. "Children ought to be able to pass them down to their grandchildren. The toys that fascinate me are the ones that existed when I was small. I love it when people come in and say, 'Oh, I had one of these,' or 'I remember this.'"

The toy shop itself is a delightful example of several nineteenth-century houses in and around Afton which Mary Ann and her husband, Maurie, have rescued and restored. (There was a time after Mary Ann and Maurie moved to Afton when rumor had it that they intended to buy up the town. "We can't afford it, and I don't think we would even have the energy, but it would be neat to keep this town in some of its original charm," says Mary Ann.)

In September, 1984, to accommodate an ever-growing clientele, Mary Ann opened a second Afton Toy Shop at Riverplace in Minneapolis. Outwardly, the two shops are look-alikes, right down to their gray clapboard with white trim exteriors. But the similarities go deeper than that. At Riverplace, as in Afton, the Afton Toy Shop is located in a historic district on what Mary Ann terms a "100%" corner. (Afton has only one commercial crossroad; Riverplace is at the intersection of Hennepin and Main where downtown Minneapolis had its beginnings.) For what it's worth, both shops have also sprouted in scenic riverside locations; while Afton fronts the St. Croix River, the Afton Toy Shop at Riverplace looks out over the Mississippi.

Felix Buckley-Jones peers through the window of the Afton Toy Shop on Afton's main street.

As far as the toys go, Mary Ann finds it hard to play favorites. "I love the Steiff toys, of course" (a reference to the German family that makes stuffed toys and teddy bears). "The bunny is probably the most incredible new toy in the last thirty years." Mary Ann picks up a lifelike arm puppet made by Steiff that sells for sixty-five dollars. "It's a really creative toy, beautifully done. A lot of people have copied it, but nobody can touch it."

Lining the doll cases, each of the English Sasha dolls, American Effanbee Storybook dolls, bisque baby dolls, and one-of-a-kind artist's dolls is likewise special. "The secret in a good doll is in the face," Mary Ann says. "Most good dolls are designed by artists or are reproductions of what artists did a century ago. There are millions of doll collectors, but the number of good dolls is limited. I'm just thrilled when I find one I think is suitable for my shops."

She also prefers wooden, not electric, trains. She had wooden trains for her own children when they were small, and now her grandchildren are playing with those same trains. "Electric trains are fine for hobbyists and for fathers, but wooden trains are wonderful for every member of the family. We've all been down on the floor helping make new layouts. You don't have to plug it in anywhere and it will never have a broken transformer. It's all creative play."

Together with Maurie, or one or more of the couple's eight children, Mary Ann makes frequent trips abroad to shop toy fairs and meet toy makers. "We find we learn a lot about a country through its toys," she says, "partly through how it treats its children, and partly through the quality of things it has for children. We're also interested in the history of toys, the universality of toys. It's always fascinating when you come home with a seemingly new thing and know that it has existed on the other side of the world, from different material but for the same purpose, to entertain and educate the child."

Dolls, stuffed animals, and wheeled toys are examples of toys found in most parts of the world. "Balancing toys made of tin or wood or other material are another thing that show up in virtually every society." (From Africa, she recently brought back an acrobats balancing toy made of bronze.) The yo-yo is also an interesting case in point, she says. "In the Arctic, the Alaskan Eskimos make a form of the yo-yo for their children by attaching small sealskin balls to the two ends of a cord."

Which countries make the best toys? "The Japanese are the toy makers to watch," Mary Ann says. "They've taken over the auto industry, the steel industry, television, you name it. I think they'll be among the best toy makers. For now, however, if one considers the whole range of toys, the Germans still make the world's finest toys."

Many of the brightly-painted windup toys Mary Ann handles in her shops are German. Some of the others, priced less expensively but no less enchanting, are from China. "Some of these are exactly the same as things we were able to get from the Chinese before the revolution, and the prices are still low." A prancing, rearing circus horse with a performer on its back who balances twirling bars on his head costs $7.95. While the Germans tend to take themselves a little more seriously, she says, the Chinese express a delightful sense of humor and color in their toys.

Mary Ann sees a trend in the American toy industry to build better toys, but she's "agin" costly marketing methods. "What people are paying for when they buy heavily-promoted toys is packaging and name and advertising." She also pooh-poohs the idea of educational toys. "It's ridiculous," she says. "All toys are educational, even the plastic things that break. They teach a lesson!" A good toy, says Mary Ann, should be both beautiful and funny ("or have some wit to it"), pleasant to touch ("which eliminates most plastic toys"), and well-made. Its real function is to give pleasure.

The most popular toy of all, hands down, Mary Ann says, is the teddy bear. "Teddy bears are made to be loved and everybody loves a teddy bear." Some of the best teddy bears are made in this country and in Germany and Japan, she says. She also has teddy bears from China ("although I never once saw a child there with a teddy bear"). "England is great teddy bear country, too. They understand teddy bears there. The British are very good about toys."

Picking up a cuddly, saucer-eyed teddy, Mary Ann says there are a few things we can learn from these bears. "Look at this one, for instance. If you watch too much television, your eyes will look like that." She is convinced, she says, that there's a good chance that teddy bears know more than we suspect. "They look at you and you just think, oh gosh. At the very least, they're strong and silent and therefore they seem wise. They're very uncritical. They're there when you need them. They're nice, too, to carry by the leg. As you come down the stairs, they thump along.

"I just wish every child in the world had a teddy bear."

Delight's Dolls

Some of the finest dolls this side of the last century are being made in Buffalo, Minnesota, by twenty-one-year-old Delight Sporre. Delight is a self-taught artist who makes both reproduction antique dolls and her own one-of-a-kind sculptured original dolls. At a recent doll show in Chicago, Delight showed sixteen reproduction dolls and came home with fourteen blue ribbons.

Having heard this much, Charlie still wasn't particularly interested in photographing dolls the day we drove out to Buffalo to meet Delight. It was a balmy day in mid-winter (with the temperature in the low forties), and all he wanted to think about was trout. If he couldn't be out catching them, he could at least be at home painting them. Getting out of the car, he hung around outside the house for a few minutes, petting the dog.

The reproduction dolls Delight showed us, the ones that are making a name for her, are exquisite copies of antique European bisque character dolls that date to the turn of the century—French Long Face Jumeau dolls, for instance, and German Hilda dolls. (These were the kinds of dolls that the lucky offspring of well-to-do parents found under their Christmas trees, even in Minnesota, in years past. Most of them were sold through mail order catalogs and some were displayed in dry goods stores.) Delight's reproductions are faithful replicas of these heirloom dolls, down to the last dimple, and more. For all they owe to earlier artists, her dolls have a freshness and vitality that is uniquely their own.

What it takes on Delight's part, for one thing, is hour upon hour of careful work. She pours the heads, hands, and feet for her reproduction dolls from liquid porcelain, using plaster molds. When this sets up into greenware, she cleans and fires each piece (at which time it becomes porcelain). The painting is done in four steps (the flesh tone goes on first while the eye lashes are saved for last), and the pieces are fired after each step. If it's a German doll that's taking shape, it gets blown glass eyes; French reproduction dolls are provided with European paperweight eyes that cost Delight fifty dollars a pair from a doll supply house. Each doll is fitted with a wig of human hair or one that Delight makes from English mohair.

Besides reproduction dolls, Delight also sculpts her own one-of-a-kind dolls, many of which tend to be fanciful creations. The first one she attempted, inspired by the movie *Star Wars*, was a Yoda doll. This went to a young cousin of hers in Texas and proved so popular that she made several more for family members and customers. She has also made E.T. dolls, dozens upon dozens of teddy bears with individually sculpted faces, and enough elves and fairies to people several pint-sized forests. All her one-of-a-kind figures are modeled from Fimo, a soft clay that bakes at a low temperature in a kitchen oven.

Delight Sporre with a collection of her turn-of-the-century reproduction dolls.

Made by Delight Sporre, this doll is copied from one that was produced in France in the late 1880s.

Delight started making reproduction dolls when she was sixteen. About the same time she also became a serious doll collector. It all had to do with an old china-head doll she had inherited from her great-grandmother. One day her mother brought home a book about dolls from an antique shop and, lo and behold, it contained an article with photographs about the same kind of doll. Since then, both Delight and her mother have been dedicated doll collectors. Their combined collection includes more than one hundred antique dolls—bisque dolls, wax dolls, paper mache dolls, and even a few composition dolls from the Forties and Fifties.

Delight grew up on a farm that borders the Mississippi River near Big Lake, Minnesota. Her parents, Derald and Ariel Ewing, grow potatoes there. Since childhood, Delight has liked the feel of clay in her hands, and at one time she considered becoming a potter. When she decided she wanted to make dolls, her parents installed a kiln for her. Ariel Ewing sews the elaborate period clothes for her daughter's reproduction dolls, mostly from old fabrics, and an aunt makes their tiny leather doll shoes. Delight designs and hand-stitches the clothes for her one-of-a-kind dolls herself.

Three years ago, Delight married her childhood sweetheart, Michael Sporre, and they have a two-year-old son, Joshua. One of the dolls Delight is proudest of is a likeness of Joshua, made when he was a few weeks old. It is a life-size replica. (She also accepts commissions to do doll portraits of other children.) Delight works on her dolls while Joshua naps in the afternoons and after he's been put to bed at night.

When Charlie and I talked with Delight, she was completing a series of black "ghetto children." Each of the dolls is individually sculpted and no two will be alike. This is the way she really prefers to work, she says. "When I make an original, it is part of me and I like that. When people buy one of my originals, they'll never see another one like it."

By the time the light was right in the upstairs hall where Charlie wanted to photograph Delight and her dolls, he had warmed considerably to his subject. Charlie sculpts some himself, and he was taking a definite interest in Delight's work. They had exchanged information on different types of clay, and she had given him some Fimo to experiment with. For the photograph he had in mind, he asked her if she would pin up her waist-length brown hair. She wears it this way much of the time anyway, she told him.

Delight sells her dolls at her home in Buffalo, at doll shows, and through Mary Ann Scroggins's Afton Toy Shops. They range in price from $8 for a tiny, hand-sculpted teddy bear to $895 for an 1890s French reproduction doll that stands thirty-two inches tall.

Antie Clare's Doll Hospital

Yes, Virginia, there is an Antie Clare. What's more, she can mend your broken doll as good as new.

Antie Clare's Doll Hospital and Museum in Oakdale is the largest of its kind in Minnesota. All told, it houses more than four thousand dolls. About half of these are displayed in the museum; the other half, both new and antique dolls, are for sale.

In the back room, shelf upon shelf is lined with hurt dolls in various stages of repair. These are attended to by one of Antie Clare's six doll doctors, all of whom she has trained. Year round, the doll doctors, dressed in pink surgical gowns, clean dolls, restring them, restore them, and sew new clothes for them.

"Christmastime is the busiest season not only for buying dolls, but also for repairing them. One mother recently brought four dolls in to Antie Clare that had been Christmas gifts for her four daughters in years past. This year she wanted to surprise her girls by having them gussied up in pastel formals for the holidays. On Christmas morning, when the daughters came down to open their gifts, the dolls would be in a row on the mantel. It's this kind of thing that makes doll repairing so rewarding," says Antie Clare.

Antie Clare is really Clare Erickson, a doll lover and collector. Her mother was a doll collector before her, and Clare began collecting dolls in earnest about 1970. At first, she started with cloth and rag dolls because she still had a few dolls of this type from her girlhood.

"A collector very often starts with the dolls he or she had as a child," says Clare. Almost before she knew it, Clare was collecting every kind of doll she could find. (Her personal collection totals about fifteen hundred dolls, most of which are on display in the museum.) Then she started repairing dolls.

When friends and neighbors began asking Clare to repair their dolls too, she set up her first doll hospital in the basement of her home. In 1981, with her business (and collection) quickly expanding, she moved to a storefront on White Bear Avenue in St. Paul. Then in June, 1984, needing still more room, she moved a second time to her present location in Oakdale, just off Interstate 94 at Century Avenue. It's hard to miss Antie Clare's Doll Hospital and Museum from the highway; on the outside, in large black letters, it says: Dolls, Dolls, Dolls.

Collectors bring their dolls to Clare, but so do five-and-six-year-old mommies of Cabbage Patch dolls. "We try to do these overnight because most of the little girls can't bear to part with their 'babies,' " says Clare. Little girls kiss their dolls goodbye and leave them in a crib that Clare has prepared for them. When a child comes to pick up her doll, it has been repaired and put back into the crib. Clare doesn't sell Cabbage Patch dolls (because she couldn't compete with discount stores), but she clearly has a soft spot for them. "They're making 'mommies' out of our little girls," she says, "something that Barbie dolls never did."

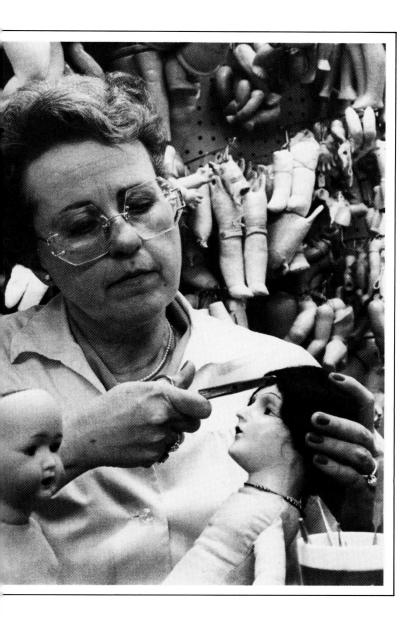

Clare buys both antique dolls and spare parts from old dolls wherever and whenever she can find them. People hear about her and bring her old doll bodies and limbs. (She also buys some new reproduction parts.) What's hard, she says, is when people come in with family dolls they want to sell. "Some of these people don't care about the dolls, but others are choking back tears."

She showed us an antique Steiff teddy bear that a man brought in recently, along with an antique doll. He wanted to know what the toys were worth, she said. When she told him they were quite valuable, he asked her if she would buy the bear. He'd like to keep the doll a while longer, he decided. The toys belonged to his wife and she was dying.

On one occasion, much to the surprise of the woman who brought it in and hadn't known its value, Clare recognized a doll as being worth sixteen thousand dollars. It was an antique French doll that belonged to the woman's mother-in-law, and she wanted it refurbished for her for Christmas.

Working from a vintage photograph, Clare dressed the doll in a copy of a gown that one of the mother-in-law's relatives had worn to a fancy-dress ball during the Lincoln administration. The fabric came from a dress the mother-in-law herself had once worn to a cocktail party for Katherine Hepburn. Clare spent long hours on this particular doll, but when her customer picked up the doll on Christmas Eve morning, she says, she wasn't a bit sorry. "The look on her face told me that my work had been worth it."

As you've probably noticed, Antie Clare spells her name minus the usual "u." It has to do with her interest in antiques, she says. Besides, she thinks "auntie," pronounced with the "u," sounds stuffy. Antie Clare is anything but stuffy. You can also trust her, Virginia, with your favorite doll.

Clare Erickson carefully trims a few snippets of hair on a Beaux Arts era French boudoir doll.

A MINNESOTA CHRISTMAS PORTFOLIO

The hexagonal tower at Fort Snelling. On Christmas Day, 1827, Lawrence Taliaferro, the Indian agent at Fort Snelling, wrote in his diary that a considerable number of local Indians, both men and women, had called on the fort "to see & shake hands & express the feelings of the day—which they appear to have taken up within the last Eight years from the Whites." He also mentions being surprised by a few "yellow kisses."

John Frankson, Marine on St. Croix, has been raising sled dogs since 1969. His teams raced in sled dogs events throughout the state (including the St. Paul Winter Carnival) for twelve years. Frankson and his dogs posed for this photo New Year's Day, 1985.

According to a Swedish friend, these Minnesota wolves are probably out gathering lutefisk for the winter. More likely, hunting in packs of two to seven animals, they'll prey on moose and deer during the Minnesota winter.

Photo by Pat Vanuga

Looking for a Christmas goose? Silver Lake in Rochester attracts some fourteen thousand wintering Canada geese each year. The reason is a nearby power plant which discharges warm water into the lake, keeping it open all winter. The geese are one of Rochester's best-known holiday attractions.

Minnesota state highway engineer Ken Kopitzke, an Afton resident, makes a hobby of building and restoring turn-of-the-century sleighs, cutters, and buggies.

A reindeer from the Minnesota Zoo poses for its picture at Riverplace, 1984.

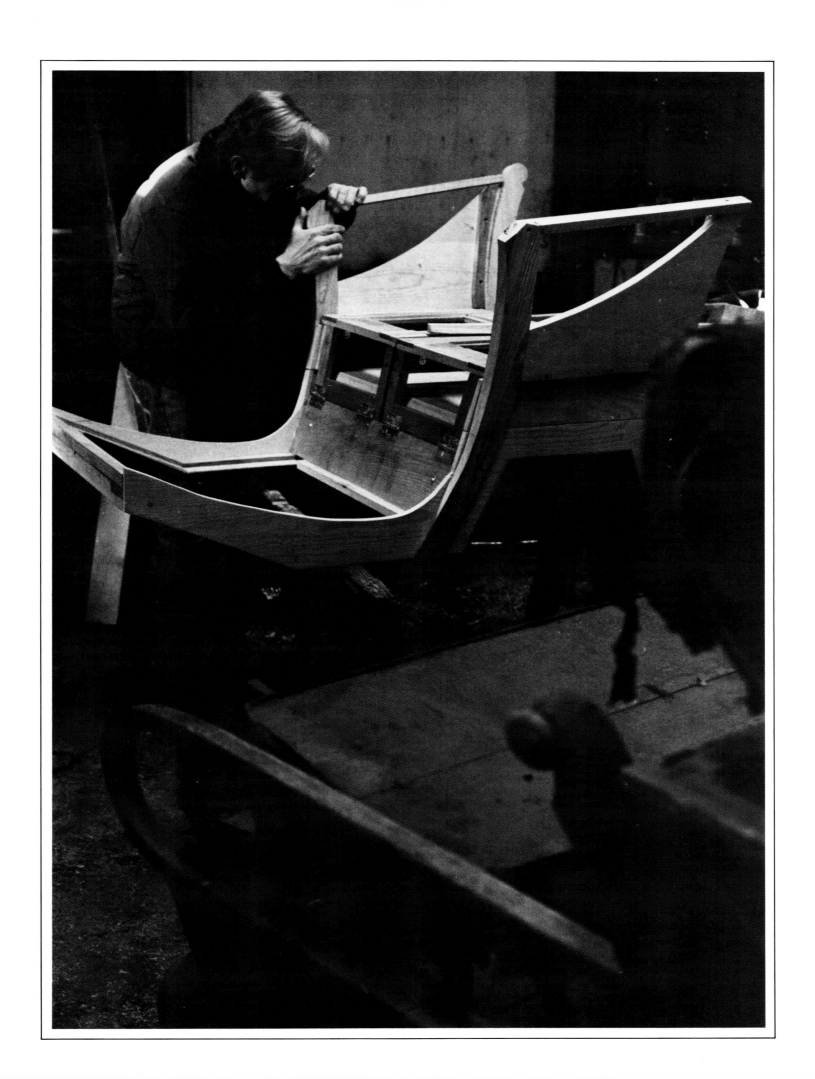

*St. Hubert's Lodge in Frontenac,
built in 1856 by Israel Garrard,
the son of a Kentucky governor, is
the only remaining example of a
French-inspired galleried residence in Minnesota. Garrard's
hospitality was legendary; the town
of Frontenac which grew up around
St. Hubert's (named for the patron
saint of hunters) became
Minnesota's first summer resort.*

A World War I soldier's grave in a cemetery at Marine on St. Croix.

The Minnesota Governor's Residence at 1006 Summit Avenue in St. Paul was built in 1912 by lumberman Horace Hills Irving and his wife, Clotilde McCullough Irving. Designed by Minneapolis architect William Channing Whitney, it was donated to the State of Minnesota by daughters of the Irvings in 1965.

Christmas Dinner at the Governor's Residence

Rudy and Lola Perpich are in Minnesota's Governor's Residence for a second time around. Perpich, who was born in the small mining town of Carson Lake, near Hibbing, Minnesota, served as the state's thirty-fourth governor from 1976 to 1978. In 1982 he was elected Minnesota's thirty-sixth governor. Delores (Lola) Simic Perpich was born in Keewatin, Minnesota.

The Perpiches celebrate Christmas with their two children, Rudy, Jr., 26 (recently admitted to the Minnesota State Bar), and Mary Sue, 24 (who received her MBA from Fordham University in New York City). Recipes for the family's Christmas dinner menu were prepared by Lola Perpich. (The turkey, candied yams, and mashed potatoes are prepared in the usual manner.)

The antipasto is a quick-to-fix version of Italian antipasto and comes from the Iron Range, says Lola. The Krumpir (potatoes) and Sarma (cabbage rolls) are adaptations of Yugoslavian recipes—bespeaking the Perpiches' ethnic background. As far as the governor is concerned, it wouldn't be a holiday without Sarma. (Beginning with Thanksgiving, Lola serves it for *every* holiday.)

"I make it as soon as the soured cabbage heads are available," says Lola. (She also explains that soured heads are made by submerging entire cabbage heads into fermenting sauerkraut. Most families on the Range used to make their own sauerkraut, she says, but now there are only a few small neighborhood markets that still do so.)

As for the two pumpkin pie recipes, Lola says: "My husband's the culprit. He is not fond of the traditional pumpkin pie, so when the family got together, he was the only one who didn't like the pumpkin pie. I found the recipe with whipped cream to suit his taste, and it has become his favorite. It's the more fattening one and the one that tastes less like pumpkin. It looks like pumpkin pie, and we call it pumpkin pie, but it only has a slight pumpkin taste."

MENU

Mock Antipasto
Cranberry Salad
Seafoam Salad
Turkey
Dressing
Candied Yams
Mashed Potatoes
Krumpir
Broccoli and Dressing Casserole
Sarma
Pumpkin Pie

Mock Antipasto   (serve with favorite crackers)

1 or 2 cans tuna, do not drain oil
1 small can mushrooms, drained
1 small bottle cocktail onions
1 small bottle stuffed olives
1 small can black olives
2 or 3 medium dill pickles, chopped
1 can sliced carrots or fresh carrots,
    sliced and cooked
1 can green beans
1 jar pickled cauliflower or fresh
    cauliflower which has been parboiled
    and soaked in pickle juice overnight.

Sauce:
1 to 1½ cups catsup
1 to 2 tbsp. wine vinegar
2 to 3 tbsp. salad oil
1 tsp. Worcestershire sauce
    salt and pepper to taste

Pour sauce, which has been beaten well, over other ingredients and fold in. Marinate for a few hours. This antipasto will keep, covered, 2 to 3 weeks in refrigerator.

Cranberry Salad

Dissolve 1 small pkg. raspberry gelatin in 1 cup hot water. Add 1/2 cup cold water. Chill until partially thickened.

Fold in:
1 can orange sections, drained
½ cup pineapple chunks, drained
¼ cup walnuts, chopped
1 can cranberry sauce (jellied or whole)

Chill until firm. Makes 8 to 10 servings.

Seafoam Salad

1 small pkg. lime gelatin
1 medium can pears
1 tbsp. salad dressing
1 3 oz. pkg. Philadelphia cream cheese
1 pt. whipping cream

Heat juice from pears; dissolve gelatin in juice. Chill until slightly set. Crush pears and add to gelatin. Cream salad dressing with cheese. Add gelatin mixture. Whip cream and fold into gelatin/cheese mixture and chill until set.

Dressing for Turkey

1 lb. ground lean pork
¾ cup butter
1 large onion
1½ cups celery
½ apple, peeled
1 small potato
1 medium carrot
2 tbsp. parsley
salt and pepper to taste
2 tbsp. sage or poultry seasoning (or to taste)
3 beaten eggs
4 qts. bread crumbs (1 large loaf bread)
1 to 1½ cups broth or enough to moisten cubed bread

Broth: Cook gizzard and neck bone with a little celery, onion, parsley, salt, and pepper in about 4 cups water for about 2 hours, adding the liver during the last ½ hour. Strain. This broth is used for the stuffing and gravy. Chicken bouillon may be added to taste if desired.

Brown the ground pork slightly in frying pan. Drain all fat. Add butter to pork. Grind the onion, celery, liver, gizzard, apple, potato, carrot, parsley, and meat from neck bones. Add this mixture to pork in pan. Salt and pepper to taste. Continue frying until mixture is cooked (about ¾ hour). Add sage or poultry seasoning. Mix. Slowly stir in beaten eggs. Pour entire contents of frying pan over cubed bread in a large bowl. Toss gently. Add enough broth to moisten all cubed bread. Mix thoroughly but gently. Cool stuffing before putting in bird.

Krumpir   ("these are excellent with Sarma")

Remove skins from boiled potatoes, dip potatoes in melted butter or margarine, and roll in corn flakes which have been mixed with a few parsley flakes. Bake in 400 degree oven for 20 to 30 minutes.

Broccoli and Dressing Casserole

1 can cream style corn
3 tbsp. milk (more if desired)
1 egg, well beaten
1 tsp. minced onion
dash pepper
salt to taste
1 pkg. chopped, cooked broccoli
½ pkg. crumb style bread dressing
1 tbsp. melted butter

Combine corn, milk, egg, onion, pepper, and salt. Add broccoli and dressing (saving some of the crumb dressing for top of casserole) and stir. Place in buttered baking dish and sprinkle with remaining dressing. Pour melted butter (more than 1 tbsp. if desired) over top. Bake ½ hour at 350 degrees.

Sarma

1 large head soured cabbage*
2 qts. sauerkraut
2 large onions, chopped
6 tbsp. butter
1 lb. ground pork
1½ lbs. ground ham
½ lb. ground beef
1 egg
1½ tsp. salt
pepper to taste
⅛ tsp. minced garlic
1 cup rice, parboiled
8 strips bacon

*Soured cabbage heads may be found at ethnic markets. If a soured head is not available, core a fresh cabbage head, and place in boiling water until the leaves soften and can be separated.

Core the cabbage and separate the leaves, rinse and drain. Wash the sauerkraut in cold water and drain. Cover bottom of large roasting pan with a layer of sauerkraut. Brown the onion lightly in butter and combine with the meats, egg, salt, pepper, and garlic. Mix well. Add the rice and mix to combine.

Place a generous portion of meat mixture on cabbage leaf, fold the sides over the meat and roll up. Layer the rolls on top of sauerkraut in roaster, adding some of the sauerkraut between each layer and ending with a layer of sauerkraut on top. Cover all with the bacon strips. Add enough cold water so the rolls are halfway submerged. Cover the pan and bake at 350 degrees for about two hours.

Pumpkin Pie   (traditional)

2 eggs, slightly beaten
1 16 oz. can solid pack pumpkin
3¾ cups sugar
½ tsp. salt
1 tsp. ground cinnamon
½ tsp. ground ginger
¼ tsp. ground cloves
1 13 oz. can evaporated milk
1 9" unbaked pie shell

Preheat oven to 425 degrees. Combine filling ingredients in order given. Pour into pie shell. Bake 15 minutes. Reduce temperature to 350 degrees and bake an additional 45 minutes or until knife inserted into center of pie comes out clean. Cool. Garnish with whipped topping if desired.

Pumpkin Pie   (the governor's favorite)

2¾ cups miniature marshmallows
1 cup canned pumpkin
1 tsp. pumpkin pie spice
¼ tsp. salt
1 cup heavy cream, whipped
baked pie shell (coconut, crumb, or plain)

Mix all ingredients except whipped cream in saucepan and cook over low heat until marshmallows are melted. Cool. Fold in whipped cream. Pour into baked shell. Chill until firm. Top with whipped cream.

Seward "Ace" Parker readies his team for a sleigh ride at Crabtree Corners, north of Marine on St. Croix. In the summer, Parker uses this same team for plowing and planting on his nearby farm.

THE SWEDISH CONNECTION

Christmas in a Sod House

In 1872 Hugo Nisbeth from Stockholm, Sweden, came to America to write a travel book. Swedish emigrants were departing for the United States in record numbers, and he intended his book for Swedes remaining behind in their homeland. Along the way, he was also anxious to meet as many of his countrymen as possible.

Shortly after arriving in Quebec, Nisbeth came straight to Minnesota where he spent two months touring the state. Liking what he saw (he was impressed with the prosperous cities and fertile farmlands; also, there were more Swedes in Minnesota than in any other state), he made up his mind to return to Minnesota for Christmas. As it turned out, Nisbeth spent the holiday with a Swedish family in a sod house on the Minnesota frontier. Later, recalling the event in his book, *Two Years in America* (1872-1874), published in Sweden in 1874, he did so with relish:

"After about a four months' absence from Minnesota [during which time Nisbeth traveled through Iowa, Nebraska, Illinois, and Wisconsin, and visited several large eastern cities and parts of Canada], I returned to 'the land of ten thousand lakes' in the middle of December, 1872. When last I was there waving fields of grain greeted my eye, and green pastures, and a happy, industrious people who joyfully turned to account the rich harvest with which the state had been blessed. Now all was changed. Winter had spread its white blanket over the fields, the trees had discarded their green dress and taken on their hoarfrost attire, sparkling in the sun."

Arriving in St. Paul (which he compared favorably to Europe's larger cities), Nisbeth found the capital city bustling with holiday activity. "The handsome stores were filled with newly arrived articles, which were tasteful and often rather costly, intended as gifts for the coming holidays. There was a brisk sale of Christmas trees in the markets and those streets along which the retailers had their shops were crowded with conveyances belonging to near-by farmers who were in town to buy gifts or delicacies for the Christmas table."

Nisbeth might have spent the holiday quite comfortably in St. Paul, but he had already made other plans. Leaving St. Paul a few days before Christmas, he took the St. Paul and Pacific train to Litchfield. "Here, after some trouble, I was fortunate enough to secure a sled in which I set out over the prairie to the west. There was no road, of course. The level country which I entered first lay like an enormous white cloth spread out before my eyes, and the only guide I had for the direction I was to take was a small pocket compass and the blue smoke column that here and there at a considerable distance arose from the log cabins.

Photo by Jeff Vanuga

Native to Minnesota, the ruffed grouse is more visible in the winter than in the summer. It is usually seen at dawn or dusk, feeding on the buds of an aspen or birch tree.

"The way was not particularly difficult to traverse, for on the flat prairie the snow distributes itself comparatively evenly. But when, after twenty or thirty miles, I came out on the rolling prairie, I met with greater difficulties. In some places the snow had drifted in considerable quantities between the hillocks, and had it not been for the hardy horses and the extraordinary strong conveyances that they have in the West, I should have had extreme difficulty in making headway."

Toward nightfall on the day before Christmas Eve, Nisbeth reached the sod house belonging to the Jan Erikson family from Wermland. The house was dug half into the ground and completed with three tiers of timbers laid above ground. It had a slightly pitched roof, and a small window had been cut in the timbers on the south side. Erikson and his wife had been in America for three years and were farming an eighty-acre farmstead. They had two children: a daughter, Anna, who was seven, and a three-year-old son, Eric. All of them were overjoyed to see someone from Sweden.

The next morning, sleeping later than his hosts, Nisbeth awoke to smell a huge ham sputtering over the fire. Outside, Erikson was busy chopping wood. Nisbeth hurried out and was met by a morning that astonished and gladdened him: "The sun was about twenty degrees above the wavy horizon of snow and from the snow-clad tops of countless hillocks the sunbeams were thrown in a dazzling bewilderment all around.... After the wood was chopped and carried in, a task in which the two children took part with a will, the cattle were fed and watered, and a small sheaf of unthreshed wheat was set out for the few birds that at times circled around the house, in accordance with the lovely old Swedish custom."

As in Sweden, the principal celebration in the Erikson household took place on Christmas Eve. "Right after twelve o'clock we were invited in by the housewife for the midday meal. The cloth that covered the plain homemade table was certainly not of the finest, but it was whole and clean, and the defects of arrangement that a fault-finding observer would have been able to point out were plentifully outweighed in my eyes by the unfeigned, cordial friendliness with which I was bade to help myself to what the house had to offer.

"For the rest, one should have felt ashamed not to be satisfied. The bread that we dipped in the kettle [in keeping with Swedish Christmas custom] was freshly baked and tasty, and the fat chicken that was later served in a sort of stewed pie form, which awakened especially the children's delight, had clearly not fared ill during the short time allotted him to live."

The Eriksons had no Christmas tree because there were no fir trees in this part of Minnesota. "But two candles stood on the white covered table and round these were placed a multitude of Christmas cakes in various shapes made by the housewife and such small presents as these pioneers were able to afford, to which I added those I had brought. Nor were *lutfisk* and rice porridge to be found on the table, but the ham which took the place of honor in their stead banished all doubt that the settler's labor and sacrifice had received its reward.

"The meal was eaten in the happiest of moods and afterward the few presents were distributed to the children. The gifts were neither costly nor tasteful, but they were *gifts* and that was all that was necessary. On the wooden horse I had brought, the little three-year-old galloped over the hard-packed dirt floor of the sod house with as much joy and happiness undoubtedly as the pampered child upon one polished and upholstered.

"All was joy and thankfulness, and when later the head of the family read a chapter from the Bible about the Christ child I am certain that from the hearts of these poor people there rose many warm thanksgivings to Him who smoothed their path and gave them courage and strength to conquer the hardships of the New World."

Concerning Christmas in general in Minnesota, Nisbeth wrote: "It is not only the Scandinavians who celebrate Christmas here… in a true ancient northern fashion, but even the Americans themselves have in late years begun to give more and more attention to this festival of the children and have as nearly as possible taken our method of celebration as a pattern. For example, most of them use fir trees with candles, confections, and other decorations, and so far as the number and costliness of the presents are concerned they often display a liberality that would amaze us Swedes. These Christmas presents are given in various ways.

"In the public schools, especially for younger children, the school officials usually arrange a huge fir, which stands for about eight days. On this tree the children's parents and friends hang small presents, which are distributed by the school-teacher. In the home the presents are sent with a message if the giver is someone outside the family, or they are distributed by a dressed-up Christmas mummer, who here goes under the name of 'Santa Claus.'

"Still another custom exists, although it is not used so commonly perhaps as the first two. If there is reason to expect presents, a stocking is hung up at bedtime in some convenient and well-known place and in it in the morning will be found the expected presents. Not a trace of our traditional lutfisk and rice porridge is found. There is no special menu for Christmas eve. On the other hand, there are few American homes in which the customary turkey is not served on the following, or Christmas, day."

*The Swedish Methodist Church,
built in Vasa in 1879, represented
the minority religious group in the
Swedish community. The church
has not been used for services since
the late 1930s and is now
abandoned, but the adjacent
cemetery is nicely tended by the
First Methodist Church in Red
Wing.*

Swan Turnblad's Castle

A second Swedish family, the Olof Manssons, came to Minnesota about the same time as the Eriksons and settled in Vasa in 1868. They changed their name to Turnblad, and the eldest son, Swan, made a name and fortune for himself as a printer. Beginning about 1900, Swan Turnblad constructed the palatial stone residence at 2600 Park Avenue in Minneapolis that today houses the American Swedish Institute.

Swan Turnblad's rise to prominence as a publisher was mostly his own doing. By the time he was seventeen, young Swan had acquired a hand press and set a 120-page arithmetic book for the principal of Lindholm's School in Vasa. Two years later, he went to Minneapolis where he worked as a typesetter. In 1887, at the age of twenty-seven, he became the manager of a Swedish language weekly, *Svenska Amerikanska Posten*. During the next ten years, he increased the paper's circulation from fifteen hundred to fifty-five thousand copies. To boot, he bought out its stockholders to become the *Posten*'s sole owner.

At the same time, Swan Turnblad was making some prudent investments. During depression years in the early 1890s, Turnblad bought into James J. Hill's Great Northern railroad. He also invested in real estate, grain, and wood pulp. Once the country's economy rebounded, Turnblad was a wealthy man. Turnblad, his wife, Christina, and their daughter, Lillian (who was an only child), toured Europe, including Sweden, in 1895, 1897, and 1899.

In April, 1900, the *Minneapolis Journal* reported that Turnblad had purchased the city's first electric automobile, a Waverly Dos-a-Dos. As it turned out, both Turnblad and James J. Hill had decided to purchase cars, and the two had a thousand dollar bet on which man would arrive home first with his auto. Not by luck, Turnblad and his car beat Hill back by three days. Turnblad had shipped his car on the railroad, while the railroad magnate drove his car home.

Swan Turnblad's newspaper boasted in large type across its front page that it was the "Biggest and Best," and this description pretty much fits the thirty-three-room stone mansion he built. Designed by Minneapolis architects Christopher Boehme and Victor Cordella in a turn-of-the-century interpretation of stately Romanesque chateau architecture, the castle-like structure was seven years in the making. When it was completed, the house had three turrets, five chimneys, fourteen flues, three sets of stairs, a third-floor ballroom, and a Moorish sitting room inspired by the Alhambra.

Herman Schlink, a master craftsman of German extraction who had studied at the Chicago Art Institute, did all the exterior stone carving as well as the interior plaster decoration. Reportedly, Turnblad asked Schlink to make the lions' heads on the gables of the house as grotesque as possible. Inside, eighteen wood-carvers worked two years to complete the intricately-carved oak, walnut, and African mahogany woodwork.

Swedish Christmas table setting in the dining room of Swan Turnblad's former residence. The carving above the fireplace depicts an ancient Swedish legend: trolls or elves could supposedly lure humans, especially fair maidens, from their earthly homes and cause them to live a life of splendor in an enchanted world.

Grand Hall staircase at the American Swedish Institute in Minneapolis. The two-story Grand Hall is paneled and decorated in African mahogany and is considered to be one of the finest such installations in the United States.

This griffin is one of a pair of wood carvings that Swan Turnblad commissioned to complete his grand staircase. Half lion and half eagle, the griffin appears in many Swedish coats of arms. The extended paw in this case indicates hospitality.

The Oriental-style rugs still in use at the Institute were made of Swedish wool in Austria because there were no looms large enough in Sweden to make them without seams. Turnblad even ordered sixty place settings of china in a royal blue and 24-carat gold design with his name and address on the back of each piece.

The Turnblads moved into their fine new residence in 1907, but it is questionable that they were ever happy there. Rumor had it that Christina was uncomfortable in the mansion—that it was too large. She and Lillian frequently traveled abroad; when they returned, the family occupied rooms on the second floor. The house rarely had any visitors, and the Turnblads shunned publicity. In 1918 the family moved across the street into an apartment building.

In 1929 Swan Turnblad gave his castle (which had stood vacant for fifteen years) to the Swedish community. The American Institute of Swedish Arts, Literature and Science (later the American Swedish Institute) was formed to administer the house, and Turnblad was its first president. "It has been my lifelong ambition to foster and preserve Swedish culture in America," he said. His gift included the residence, the three-story Posten building downtown, the Swedish newspaper, *Svenska Amerikanska Posten*, and Turnblad's collections of books and artwork.

Lillian Turnblad revealed later that her mother had insisted that the family's property be divided into three parts before her father made his gift. What Swan Turnblad gave to the Institute came out of his own one-third. When Christina Turnblad died in 1929, her estate went to different purposes, including a bequest to the Minneapolis Art Institute.

Lillian Turnblad never married. After her father's death in 1933, she went to live at Holy Angels Academy in Minneapolis. Lillian had been educated in Catholic schools, and Sister Charitas, the mother superior at Holy Angels, had been a girlhood friend. For some years afterwards, Lillian returned frequently to the Institute and worked in the walnut-paneled second-floor library, cataloging her father's books.

Christmas is observed in the best Swedish tradition at the American Swedish Institute. The Christmas tree in Swan Turnblad's immense dining room is decorated with candles, straw ornaments, heart-shaped ginger cookies, and strung with small Swedish flags. For Swedes, the Christmas tree symbolizes the tree of life. They also relate it to the ancient ancestral tree. (At one time, every Swedish farm had a tree whose growth and well-being were thought to determine the prosperity of the farm itself.) Each year the Institute also decorates Christmas trees to represent Norway, Denmark, Finland, and Iceland.

The highlight of the holiday season at the Institute is the celebration of Lucia Day on December 13. This is the first day of Swedish Christmastime. St. Lucia lived in Syracuse, Sicily, about the year 300. When she was seventeen years old and engaged to be married, her mother became critically ill. If God

would spare her mother, she promised, she would use her dowry to buy food and medicine for the Christians in the catacombs. Her prayers were answered, and Lucia distributed her gifts to the persecuted followers of Christ, tying candles on her head to light her way through the underground caves.

Lucia was later tortured and executed by the Romans, but word of her goodness spread throughout Christendom. She was canonized by the early church and Dante praised her as the "One of the Supernal Light." According to Swedish legend, during a famine in the western part of the country, Lucia crossed Lake Vanern one night in a large ship and distributed food to the starving people at different points. Standing in the bow of the boat, she wore a white robe and there was a crown of light in her hair.

Curiously enough, predating Christianity, the pagan Vikings also celebrated December 13. It was the longest night of the year by the old calendar and marked the beginning of brighter days to come. With the sun the foremost of the gods, great feasting took place to welcome back its hallowed light. Ultimately, this pagan festival became a Christian one. The word Lucia can be traced to the Latin word *lux* meaning light.

During the current century, Lucia morning is celebrated in virtually every Swedish church, club, and school. In many Swedish homes, the oldest daughter of the household assumes the role of St. Lucia and treats her family to breakfast in bed.

Public Lucia ceremonies, including the one at the American Swedish Institute, begin with a procession led by a young woman chosen to be Lucia, who dresses in a white robe (symbolizing purity) with a red sash (for charity) and wears a crown of candles on her head. She is accompanied by white-clad attendants, the girls wearing glitter in their hair and the boys wearing tall paper cones with stars on them. All sing the traditional Lucia carols.

Lucia Day Breakfast

In Scandia, Minnesota, Lucia Day services are celebrated before dawn in the community's first log church (unheated and lit only by candles), dating to 1856. Afterwards, the congregation gathers across the road at the Swedish Evangelical Elim Lutheran Church parish hall for Lucia morning breakfast.

Herring is always on the menu, along with several cheeses such as Colby and Hvarti, assorted breads including Julekage, rye bread, flatbread, and cardamom bread, also fruit soup, rice pudding, pepparkakor (ginger cookies), and Lucia buns. Lots of strong hot coffee rounds out the breakfast.

A typical Lucia breakfast served at home by the oldest daughter portraying Lucia would include Lucia buns, pepparkakor, and coffee. Rye bread, flatbread, and cheese might also be served.

Lucia Buns

2 pkgs. active dry yeast
¼ cup warm water
¾ cup lukewarm milk
½ cup butter or margarine,
  softened
½ cup sugar
2 eggs
½ tsp. ground cardamom
½ tsp. powdered saffron
  (or saffron strings)
1 tsp. salt
5 cups flour
½ cup raisins
1 egg
1 tbsp. water
2 tbsp. sugar

Dissolve yeast in warm water. Stir in warm milk, sugar, butter or margarine, eggs, cardamom, saffron, salt, and 3 cups flour. Beat until smooth. Add enough flour to make dough easy to handle. Knead dough on lightly-floured surface until smooth. Placed in greased bowl, cover and let rise until doubled. Punch down and divide into 36 parts. Roll into rope and twist the ends into an S shape. Place a raisin in each coil. Place on greased cookie sheet, brush tops with margarine and let rise until doubled. Brush with egg and water mixture. Sprinkle with sugar. Bake at 350 degrees for 15 to 20 minutes. Makes 36 buns.

Swedish Rye Bread

2 pkg. active dry yeast
¼ cup warm water
2 cups rye flour
2 cups white flour
2½ cups lukewarm water
½ cup shortening, melted
½ cup molasses
¼ cup dark corn syrup
¼ cup white sugar
¼ cup brown sugar
1 tsp. salt
3½ to 4 cups white flour
1 tsp. anise seed, crushed (optional)

Dissolve yeast in ¼ cup warm water. Stir together the flours, water, melted shortening, and dissolved yeast. Add molasses, syrup, sugars, salt, and anise seed. Beat with mixer, then by hand add the rest of the flour, kneading thoroughly. Let rise in warm place until double in bulk. Divide into 3 pieces and shape into round or traditional loaves. Let rise in pans. Bake at 350 degrees for 40 to 50 minutes.

Pepparkakor

½ cup sugar
½ cup shortening (lard)
½ cup molasses
1 tbsp. baking soda
1 tbsp. ginger
¼ tsp. cayenne pepper
2 tsp. white vinegar
1 egg, slightly beaten
3½ cups flour

Heat to boiling, sugar, shortening, and molasses in large pan, stirring constantly. Remove from heat; stir in remaining ingredients. Cover and refrigerate at least two hours or overnight. Heat oven to 350 degrees. Roll dough ⅛" thick on lightly-floured surface. Cut into desired shapes with floured cutters. Place cookies on lightly-greased baking sheets. Bake until firm, 8 to 10 minutes. Cool on wire racks. Decorate with frosting if desired.

SPEAKING OF BOOKS

A Bookman's Holiday

Bookseller Harold Lensing has been a special person in Charlie's life, and mine, for a long time. More than that, he is an institution in downtown St. Paul.

Harold opened his first book shop in 1949 on Jackson Street between Kellogg Boulevard and Fourth Street (where the Federal Courts Building is now). In 1965 Harold's Book Shop moved to its present location at 186 West Seventh Street, just south of Seven Corners. This Seventh Street shop is where Charlie and I do much of our Christmas shopping, particularly for each other.

Harold doesn't make a lot of fuss about Christmas at his shop. He just isn't interested in commercializing the holiday, he says. "The big stores uptown do enough of that." One year, he thought he'd have coffee and cookies in the store the Saturday before Christmas, but "hardly anybody came in and the coffee got cold."

Times have changed during the thirty-seven years he's been in business, Harold says. He doesn't get as many special requests at Christmas as he once did. He remembers one year when a regular customer, a railroad executive, called and wanted eight copies of *A Wedding Gift* by John Tanner Foot to give to his friends for Christmas. Harold only had one copy on hand, but he placed an ad in a bookmen's journal in New York and came up with the other seven in time for Christmas.

"They came one from here and one from there and at different prices—three dollars, five dollars, seven dollars," says Harold. "My customer didn't care. He was happy to get them all. That was some time ago when five dollars was more money than it is today. Most of the time, though, holiday patrons are apt to be looking for better editions of good books, a Dicken's classic, for instance, or a good edition of Plato."

One of Harold's favorite Christmas books is *A Christmas Carol* by Charles Dickens. "Do you remember when Lionel Barrymore used to recite *A Christmas Carol* on the radio?" he asks. "I used to enjoy that every year. He had such a good voice that you could almost see the story. He was able to change his voice enough so that you'd think there were different people there."

If it's an out-of-print book you're looking for, ask St. Paul bookseller Harold Lensing.

Harold has seen the Guthrie production of *A Christmas Carol* and agrees that it was probably well done. "But it's hard for me to get used to these modern stages that they have now. You know, where it sticks right out. I don't go to plays much anyway because it's too hard to hear. My hearing is poor, the voices don't carry, and I miss words and whole sentences."

Charlie has shopped at Harold's since he was a teenager and Harold was on Jackson Street. "Harold's feels like what I think an antiquarian bookstore should feel like," he says. "He always seems to have good things and he takes good care of his books." (Given his druthers, of course, Charlie would choose to spend most of his winter snug inside an old book shop.) According to Charlie: "If you can't go fishing or hunting or traveling, the next best thing is to visit an old bookstore. It's a treasure house."

Harold says he buys about ten thousand books a year. Over thirty some years, this comes to several hundred thousand books he's handled. Each year he sells about seventy-five books for every hundred he buys, so he has acquired a mountainous inventory. This large inventory is the main reason collectors from all parts of the country and Europe make Harold's Book Shop a regular stop.

"There was a fellow in here one day from England who wanted a certain biography of a famous English attorney," says Harold. "He told me, 'Every town I go to I look for that book. Have you got it?' I said, 'Yes,' and I walked over to the shelf and handed it to him. He couldn't believe it."

Harold is seventy-seven years old this year, and he sometimes talks about selling his shop and retiring. He'd like to have more time for skiing in the winter. Summertimes, he gardens and keeps fit on his bicycle. (When the weather's good, he rides his bicycle downtown to work.)

But for what it's worth, Harold, Charlie and I and a lot of other collectors aren't looking forward to the day you close up shop. It will be the end of an era.

Note: It is only fair to mention that Charlie and I are also partial to several other used book dealers in the Twin Cities area. These include Jim and Mary Laurie Booksellers on Snelling Avenue in St. Paul; Booksellers Et Al (Ruth McKee and her daughter, Ann McKee, Steve Anderson, and Virg Viner), also on Snelling Avenue in St. Paul; Leland Lien's Book Shop on South Fourth Street in downtown Minneapolis; and The Book House owned by Jim and Kristen Cummings in Dinkytown on the University of Minnesota campus.

Owen Jones, three-and-a-half years old, at the Red Balloon Bookshop in St. Paul.

The Red Balloon Bookshop

"Every child should have a personal library of his or her own books," says Michele Poire. "It fosters a love of reading."

Just before Christmas in 1984, Michele and her partner, Carol Erdahl, opened the Red Balloon Bookshop for children (of all ages) at Grand and Victoria in St. Paul. It is the only shop of its kind in Minnesota and one of the largest and best-stocked in the country.

"The Red Balloon is the title of a book and a movie, and the book can be read on many levels," Michele explains. "It's also a fanciful and frivolous-sounding name that's non-age-discriminatory. We want to appeal to all ages. We recently had a customer in his twenties who purchased a copy of *The Red Balloon* for an adult friend, and he wanted a balloon to go along with it." (Speaking for the shop's success, the red balloons given free with purchases have become caught in the rafters in stores and restaurants for several blocks on either side of the Red Balloon.)

Both women came up with the idea of a children's bookstore independently but at about the same time. Michele also owns the two Odegard bookstores in St. Paul. Until she took a five-year leave to open the Red Balloon, Carol was an elementary school librarian in Roseville. When friends of Carol's told her that Michele had plans similar to her own, she called Michele. The result was the Red Balloon, and it is everything the two hoped it would be.

The Red Balloon stocks a full range of children's books from A-B-C and 1-2-3 books to this year's award-winning fiction. Its non-fiction fare takes in history, biography, religion, sports, art, music, and the sciences. There are reference books (including dictionaries and atlases) and foreign language books in French, Spanish, German, Norwegian, Swedish, Russian, and Latin. And there's more besides books to this shop.

The Red Balloon also exhibits and sells original illustrators' art (paintings and drawings that are published in some of the books they carry), and book-related toys and games. There are Wednesday morning story hours for pre-schoolers, and special events, including author signings, on Saturdays for older children and adults. In the evenings, seminars for adults wanting to learn more about children's literature have been well-attended. During the past year, the Red Balloon even sponsored a kite clinic. "Like books, kites are something that raise the spirit," says Carol. "We try to provide things that will be interesting for both children and adults."

"The Red Balloon is interrelated with the whole children's book community in Minnesota," says Michele. The Kerlan Collection at the University of Minnesota, for instance, is an internationally-known resource, but it is used primarily by students of children's literature. This state is also home to many gifted children's writers. (Minnesota is really a hotbed for creativity in literature, children's as well as adult's, says Michele.) The Red Balloon is drawing on these same scholars and authors for its seminars. "We want to get some of that information out of the halls of ivy and into the homes," says Carol.

"It's important to know how to choose a good book," says Carol. "There are certain standards or criteria we use. Style and presentation and format are all important considerations. Some books are better written than others, and some have better themes, or themes that are more appropriate for a certain age or interest level. For example, a first-grader who is reading at a sixth-grade level won't be interested in a book dealing with boy-girl relationships.

"With non-fiction, you also have to know if the information is correct. Jean Fritz is an author who has done a number of well-researched biographies for children, and she does them in a delightful way. (*And Then What Happened, Paul Revere*, and *Where Do You Think You're Going, Christopher Columbus* are two of her titles.) She comes the closest to being the Barbara Tuchman of children's literature. There's also Leonard Everett Fisher who both writes and illustrates his books. He's done quite a few good historical books for children."

Parents today are very discriminating when it comes to what they want their children to read, Carol says. "They want quality books, and we provide the breadth of what's available." *Tom's Midnight Garden*, one of Carol's favorites, is a good case in point, she says. "This book was published in the 1950s in England and received the Carnegie Award (comparable to our Newberry Award which is given annually for the best contribution to children's literature). It's a marvelously fine book, but we've had people tell us, 'You're the only book-store that has it.' Yesterday I sold three copies."

"A lot of the things we recommend for Christmas are family read-alouds," says Michele. (Michele, incidentally, has been reading to her son, Peter, since he was two weeks old.) "We have several families who get a new read-aloud each year to read together in the evenings during the holidays. It's a wonderful tradition."

Pop-up books are also better-than-ever and very popular, says Carol. "Pop-ups have been around for a long time, but many of the new books are really state-of-the-art. Some of them, *The Sailing Ships* and *The Human Body*, for example, are produced for adults as well as children. There are people who collect pop-up books as well as children who delight in them."

In her own family, Carol adds, books are a staple each year at Christmas. "Each family member receives at least one book. I think that more and more people are giving each other books. Of course, as booksellers, we think that's just fine."

Carol Erdahl and Michele Poire
opened the Red Balloon Bookshop
in time for Christmas, 1984.

Wake Up, Bear . . . It's Christmas!

Charlie and I first saw the illustrations for Stephen Gammell's delightful book, *Wake Up, Bear... It's Christmas!*, at the Red Balloon Bookshop. They were hanging in the gallery area where the shop has its story hours. Gammell both wrote and illustrated the book, and it is a fetching story, in any case. Add his imaginative and bright watercolors and you have an appealing Christmas package.

Wake Up, Bear... It's Christmas! concerns Bear, a likable, large brown bear who decides he doesn't want to sleep through another Christmas. Holing up in a tree for the winter, he sets his alarm clock for Christmas Eve, then snuggles down under his blanket. On Christmas Eve, waking up and remembering what day it is, he goes out into the forest and brings home a Christmas tree. He just finishes decorating it when there is a knock at his door. Outside is a small, cold stranger, dressed in red (and with wire-rimmed spectacles suspiciously like Gammell's). Bear is about to have the Christmas of his life.

"Bear is a lot like me," Gammell says. "He's very content to be by himself. I'm sort of like that. He's all alone and he's happy being alone. Except if someone knocked on my door, I probably wouldn't answer it."

Gammell lives in Minneapolis and has been illustrating children's books for the past dozen years. Only he doesn't call them "children's" books. "I don't like that phrase. I think a lot of artists would agree. It suggests that these books are for children only. I don't think of my work as just having appeal for kids or young children." He doesn't know the exact number offhand, but he has illustrated about thirty books (including *Where the Buffaloes Begin*, which was chosen a Caldecott Honor Book). Of these, besides *Wake Up, Bear*, he also wrote *Once Upon MacDonald's Farm* and *Scudder*.

Growing up in Iowa, Gammell drew pictures like any other kid, he says. He's just never stopped. Except for an art class in high school, he is self-taught. Once upon a time, as he tells it, a friend was going to New York, so he went along for the ride and took a portfolio of his drawings with him. He wasn't really looking to get into the business, but he got work. Since then, he's had book illustration commissions from most of the major publishing houses in New York.

His second-floor studio (a large, airy room he rents in a red brick commercial building on University Avenue in St. Paul) is sparsely furnished and surprisingly neat. Except for a few of his drawings tacked here and there and a Fritz Scholder poster, the white walls are bare. "I feel freer if there's less to look at," says Gammell. "White space is important to me. I've got too much stuff on the walls as it is."

"So they sat, Bear and his visitor, talking about the snow and the wind, singing a few tunes, and enjoying Christmas Eve." This painting by artist Stephen Gammell is one of a couple dozen watercolor illustrations in Gammell's book, Wake Up, Bear. . . It's Christmas!

He keeps regular hours during the week, beginning about 8:30 or 9:00 in the morning and working well into the afternoon. "I don't wait for an inspiration and then dash over. I'm over here and I put in my time every day. I don't remember flashes of inspiration ever. When I'm in front of a piece of paper, things just happen."

Given a choice, he says he prefers working in pencil. (Most of his book illustrations have been black-and-white pencil drawings; *Wake Up, Bear* is one of only two books he has done in watercolor.) When Charlie and I visited him, he was completing the illustrations for a new book, *The Relatives Came*, in colored pencil. This was because the publisher had specified full color.

Gammell's quite happy to be where he is at the moment. Illustrating books is "fun," he says. "Sometimes I get frustrated with the pressure of doing this for a living, but on the other hand, I can never come up with anything I'd rather do. Basically, this is pretty neat."

Looking back on his own childhood, he says he always had fun at Christmastime. "I still do. I suppose that unconsciously crept into *Bear*. What I liked most about Christmas was the filled stocking—not the presents under the tree, or the tree, but the stocking. I remember coming downstairs three or four or five times a night, just peeking around the corner and looking at that big, lumpy stocking. It was more fun than opening it, actually, just looking at it there in the moonlight, leaning against the chair."

Before we left, Gammell showed us his favorite illustration from *Wake Up, Bear... It's Christmas!* Bear is strumming his guitar, humming a tune, and sitting back on his blanket inside his tree enjoying Christmas Eve. He has hung up an old stocking by the window. The painting reminds him of himself, says Gammell. He has it framed, and every year he takes it home and hangs it up for Christmas.

A Christmas Reading List

The following is a list of Christmas books, compiled by Michele Poire and Carol Erdahl, the Red Balloon Bookshop, to delight all ages. These are old books and new books, for the young and not so young:

A Certain Small Shepherd by Rebecca Caudill. Illustrated by William Pene du Bois. Holt. (Jamie, a seven-year-old mute boy speaks for the first time after witnessing a birth at Christmas.)

The Little Drummer Boy by Katharine Davis, Henry Onorati, and Harry Simeone. Illustrated by Ezra Jack Keats. Macmillan. (A favorite Christmas song illustrated by an award-winning artist.)

The Clown of God by Tomie dePaola. Harcourt. (Adapted from a French legend, the tale tells of the miracle that happens when an old juggler offers his talent to the Christ Child.)

A Christmas Carol by Charles Dickens. Many editions. (A favorite of ours is the one illustrated by Trina Schart Hyman. Holiday House.)

Wake Up, Bear...It's Christmas! by Stephen Gammell. Lothrop. (A young bear wakes from hibernation to experience Christmas. Lively, spirited illustrations.)

The Story of Holly and Ivy by Rumer Godden. Illustrated by Adrienne Adams. Viking. (Christmas morning finds an orphan and a beautiful doll finding each other and a family.)

The Nutcracker by E. T. A. Hoffman. Illustrated by Maurice Sendak. Crown. (A beautiful retelling of the original tale with bold illustrations.)

Christmas in Noisy Village by Astrid Lindgren. Illustrated by Ilon Wikland. Penguin. (Set in Sweden, a story of the excitement and customs of Christmas.)

Babushka: An Old Russian Folktale by Charles Mikolaycak. Holiday House. (Colorful and dignified presentation of the Russian version of the tale of Befana.)

Twas the Night Before Christmas by Clement Moore. Many editions.

The Best Christmas Pageant Ever by Barbara Robinson. Illustrated by Judith G. Brown. Harper. (Christmas pageants will never be quite the same after reading this hilarious story featuring the Hurdmans.)

A Child is Born by Elizabeth Winthrop. Illustrated by Charles Mikolaycak. Holiday House. (Beautiful, stately paintings illustrate the Christmas story adapted from the King James version of the New Testament.)

*Joshua Tweed as Tiny Tim and
Richard Ooms as Ebenezer
Scrooge in the Guthrie Theater
production of Charles Dickens's
A Christmas Carol.*

Photo by Joe Giannetti

GOD BLESS US, EVERY ONE!

In the past ten seasons since it opened in Minneapolis in 1975, the Tyrone Guthrie's splendiferous production of Charles Dickens's *A Christmas Carol* has become part and parcel of the Minnesota Yuletide tradition. If you've ordered your tickets early, it's a showpiece you'll be able to show off to visiting friends and relatives.

Adapted from Dickens's story by playwright Barbara Field, the Guthrie version of the Christmas classic is straightforward, stylish, witty, and beautiful. Field opens with Charles Dickens working hurriedly at his (ornately-turned Victorian) writing table. Christmas Day it might be, but the author turns a deaf ear to his children's appeals that he join them downstairs; he's going to stick with this story of *A Christmas Carol* until it's finished.

What you have is a play within a play, cleverly wrapped, and Field brings it to a very satisfactory conclusion. As Ebenezer Scrooge transforms, so does Dickens (who appears between scenes, narrating this piece). By the closing scene, following Scrooge's lead, Dickens himself abandons his enterprise and succumbs to frolic. Simply put, the audience loves it.

Penned in 1843, *A Christmas Carol* was no less popular in its own day. No sooner had it been published than Dickens had a best seller on his hands. People stopped each other on the street: "Have you read it?" everyone wanted to know. "Yes, God bless him, I have," came the reply. Critic Francis Jeffrey claimed that the book had done more good than all the pulpits of Christendom. Dickens's rival, William Makepeace Thackeray, admitted he would have given a fortune to have written it.

For his part, Charles Dickens had begun the book solely for the money; it was conceived out of the very need and greed it decried. His bills were mounting and his wife was producing babies faster than he cared to acknowledge them. Following the birth of the fifth and latest Dickens child, Francis Jeffrey, he wrote: "Kate is all right again, and so, they tell me, is the baby, but I decline (on principle) to look at the latter object."

Dickens began *A Christmas Carol* in October, and he had to complete it quickly if it was to reach the bookstores in December. So with no time to take chances, he lifted the plot, including Tiny Tim, from one of his earlier efforts, Mr. Wardle's tale of Gabriel Grub ("an ill-conditioned cross-grained surly fellow... who consorted with nobody but himself and an old wicker bottle") in *The Pickwick Papers*. The new book's title came from Wardle's song at the party.

But the curious thing was the change that came over Dickens as he got into *A Christmas Carol*. The story began to excite and intoxicate him, and he worked at it feverishly. He was seen walking the streets of London, imagining his characters and waving his arms about, gesticulating wildly. By the time he was finished, friends found him ready to weep or laugh at the mere mention of the word Cratchit. The story's moral had struck home.

Photo by Joe Giannetti

As a solution to his immediate money problems, the book was a failure. Dickens insisted on expensive binding for this love child, and the first printing netted him less than three hundred pounds. On the other hand, for better or worse, it changed the world's image of him, linking him inseparably with Christmas.

When we say: "Merry Christmas!" we are merely quoting Charles Dickens.

Stephen Kanee, who will direct the Guthrie's 1985 production of *A Christmas Carol*, also directed the play in its first season at the theater in 1975. At the time, he was a rookie director, new to the Guthrie, and it was his first professional job. "I was in New York the evening I was asked to do it," he recalls, "and my first instinct was panic. But in that position, I said, 'Absolutely, of course, I'd love it!' Then I went prowling up and down Manhattan trying to find a bookstore open at 11:30 at night with a copy of the book. Because I'd never read it."

While other theaters, including the Children's Theatre locally, were already doing various versions of *A Christmas Carol* (some of them more Dostoevskian than Dickensian), Barbara Field says that she and Kanee decided to remain as true to the Dickens story as possible. "We wanted to present what we thought was the essence of the play. It should be festive and frivolous and warm. I'm a cynic, and I knew that this was partly for Guthrie coffers, but I'm also very senti-mental."

Looking back on it, the two say they had a lot of fun with the play that first year. "We called on our friends, Jack Barkla [whose magical sets are full of wondrous flying beds, pop-up doors, and ghostly fog], Jack Edwards [who designed the Victorian glad rags, straight out of Merry Old England], and Hiram Titus [who arranged the winning musical score], and we were very excited about its possibilities." But by the time the show was set to open, Kanee was having second thoughts about it.

"We really got awfully terrified at the end," he says. "Up to that time, it was one of the most complex productions that had ever been done by this theater. It's child's play now, but at the time it seemed a rather enormous feat. Then when we went into 'tech' [adding lights, sound, costumes, and special effects], we lost the play for about ten days. We spent so much time moving platforms, getting fog on the stage, getting steps to collapse, and people into the right costumes that we never really had a run-through with the play until the first preview.

"The actors were at a loss to remember what the play was about. I felt dread-fully guilty, and we all anticipated it was going to be just a hideous disaster. The preview was very, very shaky. The second preview—we only had two previews then—looked marginally better. Then we opened. None of us really had much confidence. Certainly I didn't."

*Richard Ooms as Ebenezer
Scrooge.*

Photo by Joe Giannetti

Suspended animation: this merry-go-round goat is one of several such animals in an indoor court-yard at Riverplace in Minneapolis.

84

As it turned out, Kanee needn't have worried. Audiences cheered it and so did the critics. Robert Girouard in the *Mankato Free Press* called it innovative in interpretation and technically ingenious," noting that it let the original Dickens story "shine through with unimpeded, unabashed sentiment." Don Morrison in *The Minneapolis Star* said, "I left it whistling a Christmas carol. Amazing!"

"I think the reason it worked then is the reason it still works," says Kanee. "The audience brings something to the story that causes a response in the actors to give that story back to the audience. In a funny way, it's sort of like a love affair. I think our triumph is that we never really got too much in the way of Dickens's story."

Earlier in 1972 the Guthrie had put on what the theater called a "glove and scarf" version of *A Christmas Carol*. It lacked sets and costumes (with the exception of mittens and mufflers), and all four ghosts were simply offstage voices. Nonetheless, says Sheila Livingston, the theater's public relations director, it was well-received. "But we felt that what would really be an enormous gift to the community would be to do the most wonderful production of *A Christmas Carol* that was possible. To bring to life the wonderful character of Ebenezer Scrooge.

"Barbara Field was literary manager at that time and she adapted the novel, incorporating Charles Dickens into the production. I think that really has made it a very special thing—that you have Dickens telling the story. Then with Jack Barkla designing it, and Stephen Kanee directing it, it is an extravagant production, full of color and life. From the very beginning, from the first time it appeared on our stage, the house has been full. People actually begin ordering tickets for it in April and May."

The 1985 production, with both Kanee and Field back on the scene (after a several-years absence from the Guthrie rosters), will see some changes. "We have to remember what we once did with it," says Field. In recent years, for instance, the play has been expanded until it was nearly a full hour longer than its original hour and a half format.

"I don't think the story can sustain that length," says Kanee. "What we plan to do is get it back into the original mold. We also expect to have a much stronger cast. We have scoured the country to put together our present repertory company, and we have the best actors that we could possibly get."

It's anybody's guess as to how many more years the play will run. "The Guthrie's production of *A Christmas Carol* has really become an integral part of the life of the Twin Cities," says Livingston. "I think people would miss it if we didn't do it. People like it because it really does have an important message—the fact that being a generous person does bring more happiness. People love to hear that story, over and over again.

"It's funny how a tradition starts, isn't it!"

Carriage rides are part of the holiday fun at Riverplace in downtown Minneapolis.

After-the-Theater Holiday Buffet

When we needed the perfect menu to cap a fancy-dress night on the town, we phoned Byerly's. Don Byerly's luxury food stores are a Minnesota phenomena—even a tourist attraction. *People* magazine called Byerly's supermarkets "the world's swankiest grocery chain;" *The Wall Street Journal* dubbed them "the Bloomingdale's of the supermarket world."

The recipes were created by Byerly's staff of home economists. Keeping in mind that the supper hour would be late, they chose recipes that are either quick-to-prepare or can be made ahead of time.

Staircase at the Pratt-Taber Inn in Red Wing. This lovely historic home, built in 1876 for pioneer Red Wing banker, A. W. Pratt, opened last year as a bed and breakfast guest house.

MENU

North Woods Apple Cider
Wild Rice Soup
Spinach 'N Strawberry Salad
Bread Sticks or Favorite Bread
Cookie Tray
Coffee   Tea

North Woods Apple Cider   "...a festive beginning"

2 cups water
½ cup brown sugar
1 tbsp. grated orange peel
2 tsp. whole cloves
1 tsp. whole allspice
¼ tsp. ground coriander
¼ tsp. nutmeg
3 cinnamon sticks
1 (64 oz.) bottle apple cider
½ cup orange juice
3 tbsp. lemon juice
1 cup light rum
   cinnamon sticks (optional)

Combine first 8 ingredients in 2 qt. saucepan. Heat to boiling, reduce heat; simmer, covered, 20 minutes. Strain through cheesecloth into 4 qt. Dutch oven. Stir in remaining ingredients; heat through. Serve in cups or mugs with a stick of cinnamon.

Amount: 20 (½ cup) servings

Wild Rice Soup   "elegant"

2 tbsp. butter
1 tbsp. minced onion
¼ cup flour
4 cups chicken broth
2 cups cooked wild rice
½ tsp. salt
1 cup half and half
2 tbsp. dry sherry (optional)
   minced parsley or chives

Melt butter in saucepan, saute onions until tender. Blend in flour; gradually add broth. Cook, stirring constantly until mixture thickens slightly. Stir in rice and salt; simmer about 5 minutes. Blend in half and half and sherry; heat to serving temperature. Garnish with minced parsley or chives.

Amount: 6-7 cups

Variation: Add ⅓ cup minced ham, ⅓ cup finely grated carrots and 3 tbsp. chopped slivered almonds with rice and salt in recipe above.

Spinach 'N Strawberry Salad   *"an unusual strawberry combination"*

12 oz. fresh spinach
2 tbsp. sesame seeds
¼ cup safflower oil
2 tbsp. salad vinegar
2 tbsp. sugar
2 tbsp. minced green onion
1 tsp. salt
  dash pepper
  dash Tabasco
1 pt. strawberries, sliced

Wash spinach, discard stems; dry and tear into bite-size pieces. Wrap in toweling, refrigerate. Toast sesame seeds on pie pan in a 350 degree oven, shaking once or twice until golden (10-12 min.); cool. Combine oil, vinegar, sugar, onion, salt, pepper, and Tabasco in covered container until sugar dissolves; refrigerate. To serve: In salad bowl, toss dressing into spinach and sesame seeds. Gently toss in strawberries.

Tip: One cup pomegranate seeds may be substituted for strawberries.

Chocolate Almond Delights   *"melt in your mouth"*

¼ cup whole blanched
  almonds
1 cup butter, softened
½ cup confectioners sugar
1 tsp. almond extract
2 cups flour
3 oz. semi-sweet chocolate
2 tbsp. butter
2 tbsp. milk
½ tsp. almond extract
1 cup confectioners sugar

Spread almonds on baking sheet, toast in a 350 degree oven until lightly browned (8-10 min.). Cool, chop, set aside. Cream butter, the ½ cup confectioners sugar, and almond extract until fluffy, blend in flour. Roll a rounded half teaspoon of dough at a time into marble-size ball. Arrange 1½" apart on ungreased baking sheets. Bake in a 350 degree oven until firm but not browned (about 10 min.). Cool. Combine chocolate, butter, and milk in a small saucepan, stirring over low heat until chocolate is melted and ingredients are blended. Stir in almond extract and the 1 cup confectioners sugar until smooth. Spread ½ tsp. filling on flat side of one cookie, lightly press on another cookie, flat sides together. Roll chocolate edge in reserved chopped almonds.

Amount: about 5 dozen

Holiday Fruit Bars   *"make in minutes"*

6 tbsp. butter
1½ cups graham cracker crumbs
1 (8 oz.) pkg. candied cherries
  or cherry-pineapple mix,
  chopped (about 2 cups)
1 cup chopped dates
1 cup shredded coconut
1 cup chopped pecans
1 (15 oz.) can sweetened
  condensed milk

Melt butter in 10 x 15" jelly-roll pan. Sprinkle graham cracker crumbs over melted butter. Sprinkle with chopped fruit, dates, coconut, and pecans. Drizzle sweetened condensed milk over all. Bake in a 350 degree oven until browned (25-30 min.). Cool; cut into bars.

Amount: 50 (1½ x 2") bars

Decorated for its first Christmas in 1984, Riverplace in Minneapolis (on the downtown riverfront) is Minnesota's most extravagant shopping mall.

Index